NXTmonitor
User's Guide

Copyright

Copyright © 2002-2021 eCube Systems LLC

Mailing Address

eCube Systems LLC
401 College Street, Suite 200
Montgomery, Texas 77356

Phone Numbers

Phone: 1 (936) 449.6877
After Hours Technical Support: 1 (866) 493.4224
Fax: 1 (936) 449.4880
Sales & Service: 1 (936) 449.6877

Email Addresses and Web Site

Marketing email: marketing@ecubesystems.com
Sales & Service: ev_sales@ecubesystems.com
Technical Support: techsupport@ecubesystems.com

http://www.ecubesystems.com

07/2021

Products and Services eCube System Offers

eCube Systems specializes in maintaining, supporting and modernizing legacy application systems. We have products and services that maximize the return on technology investment by leveraging existing technical assets to meet your evolving business needs. We provide the capabilities to reduce risk, extend ROI, and increase productivity as we consolidate legacy capabilities and evolve legacy systems to contemporary technology platforms, such as XML,.NET, J2EE, ESB and Web Services. Our Enterprise Evolution solution features the ARM process: Assessment, Remediation and Modernization.

We are leaders in implementing composite applications that enable immediate increases in business productivity while providing a smooth manageable evolution to contemporary technologies.

We offer the following products and services:

If you have a project you would like eCube Systems to undertake, please contact us.

Brief Contents

Detailed Contents

Chapter 6
NXTmonitor Mobile.. 129

Contents

Chapter 1
Introduction

This chapter covers how to use *NXTmonitor User's Guide*, who should use it, a quick rundown of topics, and a list of format conventions.

All information in this book may also be accessed by using the oechelp on-line help utility.

- "Using this Book" on page 2.

- "Format Conventions" on page 4.

- "Introduction" on page 6.

Using this Book

Welcome to the NXTmonitor User's Guide. This book introduces the server and object management functions with discussions of important topics with a step-by-step instruction to introduce you to some of the more complex features you can use when building or managing distributed applications. The Troubleshooting section identifies and describes error conditions during management of the distributed servers and the NXTera TCP servers. This book also provides a compilation of problems and error messages - and what to do about them - that you might encounter when using the eCube utilities, or coding clients and servers. Take a minute to read these two pages - make sure you have the background that we assume you have, and make sure you are reading the right book.

Who should use it

This book is designed for all developers and administrators who manage distributed applications. Whether you are responsible for building servers, scripting GUI clients, or configuration an application, this book provides a detailed understanding of how you can manage and customize applications in an open distributed environment. You should not attempt to build a custom three-tiered application until you have read this manual.

What you should already know

In general, you should have a basic understanding of client/server computing, and of the limitations inherent in two-tiered architectures. You should have read Read This First and understand the principles of Distributed Computing before delving into this manual.

Some sections of the book require you to know a scripting language.

When to use it

Through task-oriented instructions and plain-language discussions, The NXTmonitor User's Guide provides you with expanded knowledge and skills to supplement the fundamentals you learned from the Server Developer's Guide.

Refer to this book when you need to know more about certain NXTmonitor management features, such as Security and other administrative issues. This book and the Reference should provide all the information you need to understand the more advanced features or uses of the NXTmonitor Management utility.

Use the Troubleshooting section when you need information on:

- Problems you may encounter during installation.
- Problems you encounter while using the NXTmonitor features.
- Problems you encounter while developing and managing clients and servers.

Use this book as a supplement to the user guides in the NXTera documentation set.

Format Conventions

Text Conventions

Understanding the conventions used in this manual will help you to learn how to use the utilities and to navigate the manual's structure.

Format	Explanation	Example
`Terminal`	Designates the operation system or utilities, file names, or constant values for variables.	`Kermit,telnet,` `cust.def`
Sub-text	Designates text that represents many possible literal values; substitute your particular value here.	*server*_c.pl -e *environment.file*
Bold	In body text, bold designates NXTera utilities. In examples, bold highlights parts of the code.	**nxtbroker** **NXTmonitor**
`[brackets]`	Designates optional text unless a vertical bar appears inside the brackets; in this case, one of the choices is required.	[-d *def_file*] [NONE | ERROR | WARN | DEBUG]

Paragraphs set off in the following manner are code examples:

```
#include <stdio.h>

main() {

        int I;
        printf("The number is $d",i);

        }
```

Symbols

The following symbols are used throughout the documentation to help you navigate the text.

Symbol	Meaning
	**Warning Message**. Indicates that you should pay special attention to the accompanying message. The message contains crucial information, without which you will not be able to continue properly.
	**Hint Message.** Indicates that the accompanying text, while it is not crucial information, does supply you with helpful instructions, depending on your situation.
	**Optional Message**. Indicates that the accompanying text is optional. The message may outline additional functionality or an alternate method, or detail a process step that may aid you in understanding a concept.
	**Debugging Tip**. Indicates that the accompanying text contains instructions on debugging the current step of your project. Debugging tips may be skipped if you use other successful debugging methods or if you choose not to debug (at your own risk).

Introduction

NXTmonitor is a three tier application management system designed for managing distributed applications on the enterprise. There are many challenges to managing distributed computing applications and NXTmonitor lets you successfully manage them quickly and efficiently from a centralized console.

NXTmonitor helps you effectively manage your distributed applications with the use of versatile tools to keep track of various components of the distributed application: log file management and configuration changes. NXTmonitor has the ideal architecture and functionality to easily monitor your application and perform complex and routine management functions.

NXTmonitor helps you concentrate on efficiently managing your applications with these basic steps:

1. The first step in managing your distributed applications is proper configuration. The configuration of your distributed application requires some in-depth knowledge of the dependencies within the individual components. It is possible to configure your distributed application so that it is mismanaged and poor performing. In configuring your distributed application, you define the components along with the behaviors so NXTmonitor knows how to manage them.

2. Manage your distributed application. NXTmonitor lets you manage your distributed application through a graphical interface (GUI), which is known as the console. Once you start your application, you can close the console, and NXTmonitor will continue to manage your application.

3. Monitor and troubleshoot your distributed application. By continually monitoring your distributed application, NXTmonitor ensures that the application remains functioning. NXTmonitor also enables you to make changes to the structure or the configuration dynamically, empowering you to react to changes in your computing environment or potential problems as they arise. NXTmonitor lets you trouble shoot

your applications because it lets you display the contents of the log file in the console. NXTmonitor also does application fail-over and load-leveling. If your application fails, NXTmonitor detects it and restarts it.

The figure below shows the basic steps for creating an environment for managing your applications with NXTmonitor.

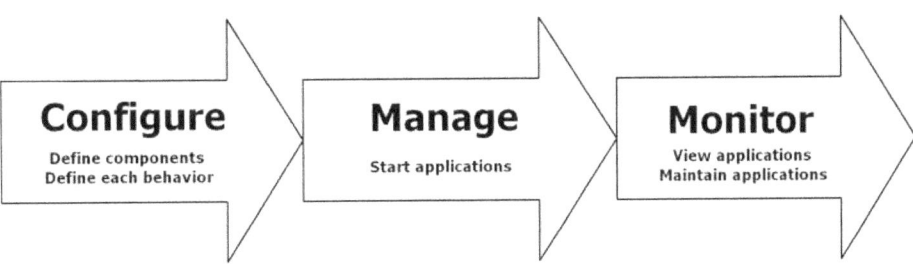

Technical Support

eCube Systems offers a variety of support options. These include free services on the Internet, where you can search our information database. In addition, you can choose telephone support or on-site consultant support. To set up an account, call our support line at 936-449-6877 or email us at support@ecubesystems.com.

System Requirements

Before you set up your environment to start managing your distributed applications, you need to determine the best computers to fit your management requirements. Putting the right software components on the right computers will ensure a smoothly running monitoring system. The first consideration in effectively managing your applications in a distributed environment is memory. Sufficient memory is the key to getting adequate performance out of these Java based tools. In addition, a relatively fast

CPU will also aid in performance of simple and more complex management tasks.

Here are some guidelines for the hardware system requirements for the Console:

1+ GHz CPU (Intel)

10 Gigabytes disk space (mostly for logs)

2 Gigabytes of memory

Software Requirements:

Sun Java JDK 1.6 or higher

Supported Platforms

As of the writing of this manual, NXTmonitor is supported on most client platforms including **Windows 2000-2008, XP, Vista, 7, MacOS X, Redhat Linux 4,5**, and the following server **Unix OS: Solaris 8, 9, 10, AIX 5.X**, and **HP-UX 10, 11**. For more current NXTmonitor system requirements, see the NXTmonitor release notes. The list below lists the OS upon which it will run without a problem:

UNIX (any - Solaris, AIX, HP-UX, BSD, IRIX,)

Windows: 2000, XP, Vista, 7, 10

Linux (any)

Mac OS 10+

Terminology

Before we begin introducing the design and structure of NXTmonitor, there are some key terms that will be used in this discussion. Accordingly, this section will define this terminology and how it relates to the NXTmonitor Application Management System.

Term	Description
Managed Object	A managed object is a distributed application that has been configured into NXTmonitor's configuration.
Console	The console is NXTmonitor's Graphical User Interface (GUI). With the console, you can configure, monitor and manage your distributed application.
Agent	The component that manages and monitors the managed objects. An agent must be installed on every computer where distributed applications will be run.
Master Server	The NXTmonitor Master Server process provides each distributed application with constant monitoring. It controls all of the managed objects associated within a configuration.
Application	Application refers to a distributed or multi-tiered application and is comprised of all of the objects, resources, pro-cesses and middleware that together constitute a working application.
Configuration	A configuration is a collection of definitions for distributed applications that are monitored and managed by NXTmonitor. The configuration contains all of the information necessary to start, stop, run, deploy, and alter the envi-ronment of managed objects in an application.

Chapter 2
NXTmonitor's Features & Capabilities

This chapter introduces NXTmonitor's features, and then explains NXT-monitor's capabilities in depth. Once you understand what a feature does, see the section on Starting NXTmonitor for how to implement it.

Before you read this section, you should already be familiar with the infor-mation provided in the Server Developer's Guide. Because NXTmonitor's main function is to start and monitor distributed applications, you should be particularly comfortable with the structure of distributed applications, including multiple Broker hierarchies.

- "Introduction to NXTmonitor" on page 12.

- "Multiple Broker Hierarchies" on page 18.

- "Architecture" on page 20.

- "Action icons" on page 22.

- "Status icons" on page 23.

Introduction to NXTmonitor

The NXTmonitor utility provides the following distributed applications management services with the NXTera Open Development Environment:

- It starts and stops services

- It manages Servers

- It manages Brokers

- It manages Objects

- It manages Timers

- It checks services at regular intervals to ensure they are running;

- If a Broker goes down, NXTmonitor restarts the Broker, and re-registers all services that were registered with that Broker;

- It contains configurable events and actions to further monitor servers.

- It provides groups for load levelling, and fail-over.

- Combined with groups, timers, events and actions, it can provide intelligent scaliability and capacity planning.

If a server goes down, NXTmonitor starts another instance of that server.

NXTmonitor's main function is to make the start-up and maintenance of NXTera applications more convenient. NXTmonitor does not have to be running in order for clients, serves and Brokers to communicate; it does, however, add considerable robustness to any NXTera application.

Summary of Features

NXTmonitor itself is a three tier application which can be distributed within an enterprise's network. It has three main components which can reside across multiple servers. This architecture allows NXTmonitor to effectively manage distributed applications through its flexible structure and distributed environment. NXTmonitor's features are briefly explained below.

Graphical User Interface

NXTmonitor's graphical user interface (hereafter referred to as its GUI or Console) makes managing your applications easy, since you can immediately see what is running. NXTmonitor Console is Java-based, so it runs on any Unix, Linux, MacOS or Windows platforms. Console screen below:

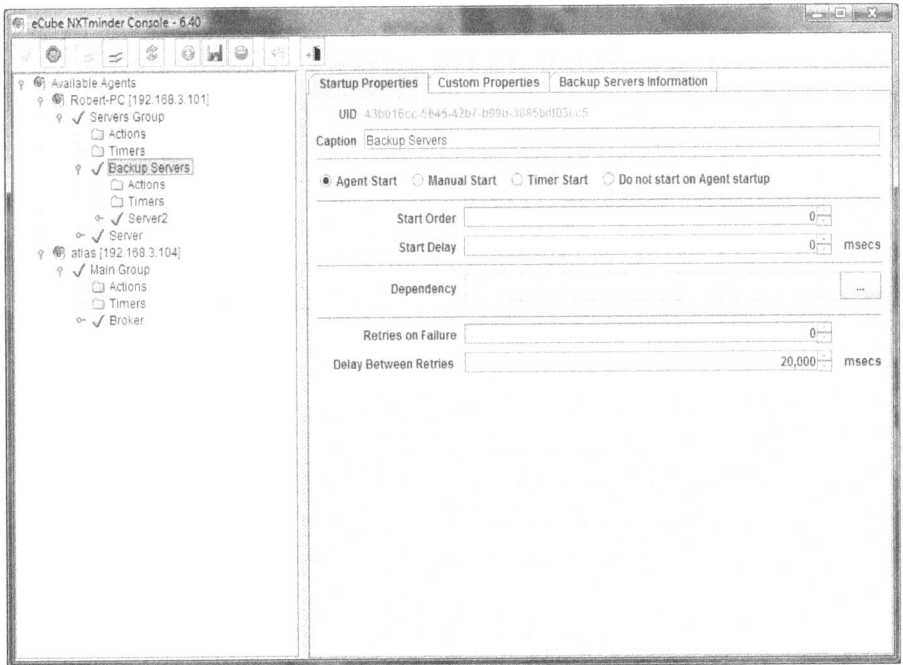

Agents

NXTmonitor uses agents to start and kill services on any machine, local or remote. An agent is a process that runs continuously in the background, waiting for another process (in this case, NXTmonitor) to contact it and request some action from it.

Whenever NXTmonitor want to start or kill a service, on any host, it sends its request to the NXTmonitor agent running on that host. The agent then executes NXTmonitor's request. Any NXTmonitor can access the NXT-monitor agent on a particular host, provided the passwords of the two processors match.

The agent communicates with NXTmonitor by using eCube's library of net-work functions, so this version of NXTmonitor can run on any network with TCP/IP support.

Master Server

The Master Server is the brains of the NXTmonitor distributed management application. The configuration file is stored in the repository managed by the Master Server and the Master Server interprets all the events, initiates actions and manages the brokers, servers and objects within this configura-tion. In addition to these functions, it also functions as an Agent. There can only be one Master Server per NXTmonitor configuration.

Internal Security

NXTmonitor includes two security features:
- Authenicated and encrypted communicaton between NXTmonitor and NXTmonitor agents.

- NXTmonitor can be locked with the same password.

NXTmonitor and its agents use a password to make sure that each is authenticated and authorized to talk to the other, and also encrypt messages using the password.

You can also use this password to "lock" and unlock NXTmonitor into monitoring its current configuration. This prevents unauthorized user from changing any parts of the current configuration.

Manages Secure Applications

Each NXTmonitor configuration must consist entirely of secure servers and Brokers, or entirely of unsecure servers and Brokers. Secure NXTmonitor encrypts passwords, Broker keys, and RPCs between NXTmonitor and its agents, using DES encryption.

Configuration files

You can use NXTmonitor's interface to create and debug the distributed application hierarchy interactively. Once completed, you can save the hierarchy configuration as a configuration file (you provide the name). You can then load this file at any time to recreate the desired setup of servers and Brokers quickly and easily.

Multiple Broker Hierarchies

In any NXTera configuration, there must always be one master Broker which keeps track of all of the servers. The master Broker can also keep track of other Brokers, called "sub-Brokers." Each sub-Broker may, in turn, keep track of its own servers and Brokers.

This multiple Broker structure has two main advantages. It minimizes the load on any single Broker by allowing more than one Broker to keep track of an application's services; this distributes the "brokering" duties among the braches of the tree. For more information about NXTmonitor monitoring multiple Brokers, see "Multiple Broker Hierarchies".

Backwards Compatibility

NXTera NXTmonitor on UNIX and Windows can load and import AppMinder configuration files, but not save them. When NXTmonitor detects that it is loading an AppMinder version of a configuration file, it converts the file to the NXTmonitor format. Net Minder configuration files cannot be converted since the old configuration file is no longer supported.

NXTera NXTmonitor cannot load an Entera DCE configuration file. The information required for the Entera DCE version of NXTmonitor is very different from that contained in a NXTera configuration file.

Error Checking

When servers and Brokers are started, NXTmonitor always generates a .log file that contains the RPC messages and logs. These services also create .err files, which contain outputs to STDOUT and STDERR from these ser-vices. These two files for each service provide most of the information needed to debug and test a distributed application.

To provide easier access to these files for the user, NXTmonitor comes with a file reading utility, called reader, that can be used while NXTmonitor is running. The reader utility allows the user to read the .err and .log files for the selected service - Broker, server even NXTmonitor itself. You can also update or re-read the file in the reader window by double-clicking the reader window.

NXTmonitor as a server

If you are using NXTera, NXTmonitor has a complete and fully-documented RPC API (Remote Procedure Call Application Programming Inter-face) that allows other processes to access all public NXTmonitor functions. This API allows NXTmonitor to function as a server, in addition to its more frequent role as a client.

The API permits users to develop clients (a load-balancer, or a NXTmonitor GUI running on Windows, for example) that access NXTmonitor functions remotely.

This feature is in compliance with the general paradigm of providing all NXTera/Entera tools with server capabilities.

Using this feature, NXTmonitor can be configured to keep track of other NXTmonitors! NXTmonitor 1 can keep track of NXTmonitors 2 and 3, each of which are keeping track of their own configurations. If NXTmonitor 2 should go down, NXTmonitor 1 can restart it, which then restart its own entire configuration. This kind of redundancy adds more robustness to NXTmonitor's distributed application functions.

Fine-tuning NXTmonitor

NXTmonitor has many options that allow the user to fine-tune its operation. These characteristics of NXTmonitor can be set on the command line, and/or modified at run time. These characteristics are listed in the table entitled "NXTmonitor command line options and default values".

Multiple Broker Hierarchies

Entera/TCP and NXTera NXTmonitor supports multiple Broker hierarchies. There must always be one mast Broker which keeps track of other services, a "service" bing defined as either a server or a Broker. Any Broker that reg-isters with another Broker is called a "sub-Broker."

Each sub-Broker may, in turn, keep track of its own services; this hierarchy resembles a tree-like structure of services with the master Broker as the root. (Keep in mind that this tree is upside-down, similar to a family tree.)

Figure: 3.1 A Multiple Broker Hierarchy

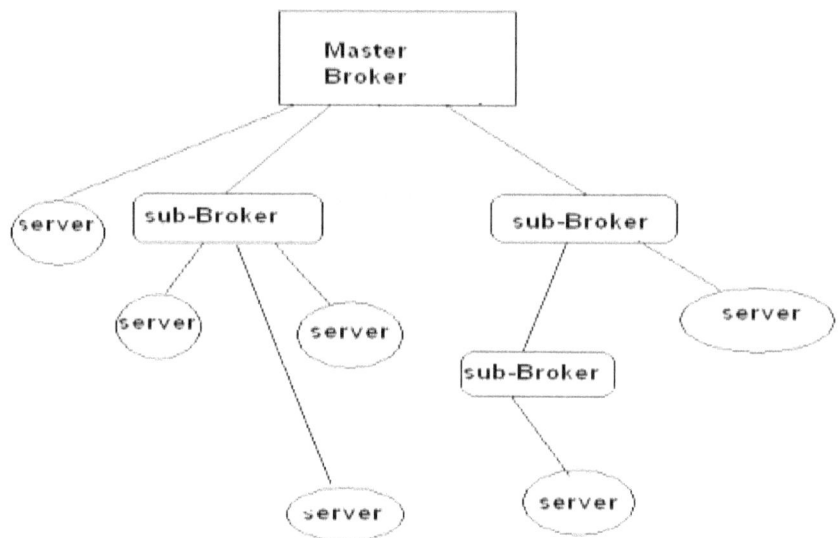

On NXTmonitor's list of services, the first Broker is called the `Master Broker`, and all others are called `rpcbroker`.

Advantages

Minimize Load

This multiple Broker structure has two main advantages. It minimizes the load on any single Broker by allowing more than one Broker to keep track of an application's services, this distributes the "brokering" duties among the branches of the tree.

Consider the following example. Company A has an application that consists of twenty-one servers. The application administrators can distribute the load of these servers by starting a master Broker with four sub-Brokers. Each of the sub-Brokers can then keep track of several servers - say 4 servers are tracked by sub-Broker 1, 4 by sub-Broker 2, and 6 and 7 by sub-Brokers 3 and 4 respectively.

Robustness

The second advantage is robustness. In a multiple Broker structure, if one of your many sub-Brokers were to become unavailable for any reason, NXTmonitor still has access to other sub-Brokers.

Hint for Administrators of Distributed Applications. You can duplicate the entire structure of a master Broker - sub-Broker-server hierarchy so that two NXTmonitors each keep track of an identical set of the functionality of an application. Another NXTmonitor can monitor both identical NXTmonitors, and if anything happens to one set, the other set continues to provide functionality, assuming the load of the set which is down.

Architecture

NXTmonitor is itself a distributed application comprised of three components that can reside across multiple computers. This design allows NXTmonitor to effectively manage distributed applications. The three components of NXTmonitor are:

- **The Master Server** - only one per configuration and contains agent functionality.

- **Agents** - one per computer where objects are managed.

- **The Console** - the GUI interface to NXTmonitor (example below):

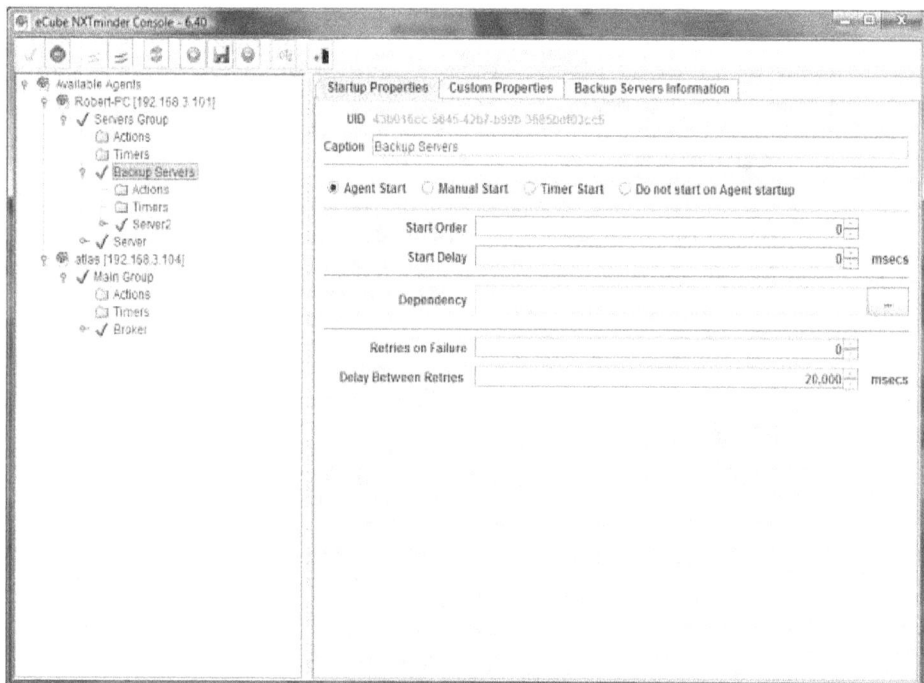

Master Server

The NXTmonitor central management functions and key to managing applications resides in the Master Server also known as the NXTmonitor Server or the Monitor. The master server provides the primary management con-trol of the managed objects with several managed services that monitor and maintain the health of these running applications. The Master Server usu-ally runs in tandem with multiple agents, sending information to each based on timers or commands it receives from the console. In order to han-dle deployment on multiple computers, an agent service must run on every system being managed including the one upon which the Master Server runs. Accordingly the Master Server contains both the management logic and the agent logic. The mode is determined at the installation time.

Note: *When the Master Server is installed on a system, an Agent is not necessary and will generate an error if you attempt to install an Agent on the same machine as the Master Server.*

Agent

The second component is the Agent, which does the majority of the ser-vices or object-related tasks for NXTmonitor. The Agent is also written in Java, and can operate on virtually any Operating System to manage serv-ers/objects on that OS. With its agent architecture, NXTmonitor can manage almost any type of application object on virtually any platform that can support a JVM. In order to launch processes on different computer sys-tems, NXTmonitor needs to have the agent installed on each. The agent pro-cesses commands from the Master Server and it can dynamically load launcher modules to manage and monitor objects. Each agent contains spe-cific command launchers for starting, stopping and monitoring of managed objects in configurations for a specific server (computer). The agent can be copied to each computer where applications are to be launched and man-aged by ftp or cross mounted with NFS.

Console

The NXTmonitor console is the central Graphical User Interface (GUI) for managing NXTmonitor controlled services and objects in an enterprise environment. The Console is also a Java application using Swing compo-nents and is the primary source of information for management. The Console GUI is laid out for maximum information display to the analyst and provides instant recognition when problems occur. The layout is a classic three pane layout with menu items and action buttons on the top header of the GUI.

Action icons

There are two main types of icons used in the NXTmonitor Console. The first kind is the action button icons, whose functions and descriptions are listed in the table below:

Icon	Function
	Add: Add a server or component to the managed configuration
	Remove: Remove a server or component from the configuration
	Refresh: This button will refresh the console image; used in cases where a status change is expected
	Reload: This button will reload the Agents tree
	Save: This button is used to save changes to the configuration
	Start: This button brings a server or group up

Icon	Function
	Stop: This button brings a server or group down
	Disable: This button disables a server or group (gray)
	Enable: This button enables a server or group (blue)

Status icons

The left side of the main panel is the navigation frame and it displays a tree structured representation of the NXTmonitor configuration being managed. The status icons used in this frame indicate the status and are explained below:

Icon	Function
	Master Agents: Master Agents Manager
	Master Agent: Master Agent Node
	Agent: Agent Node
	Master Group Starting: Indicates the master group is starting.
	Master Group Started: Indicates the master group is started
	Master Group Stopping: Indicates the Master Group is stopping.
	Master Group Stopped: Indicates the Master Group is stopped.

Icon	Function
	Master Group Failure: Indicates the master group has failed to start.
	Master Group Disabled: Indicates the master group is disabled. (gray)
	Master Group Enabled: Indicates the master group is enabled.
	Group Starting: Indicates the group is starting
	Group Started: Indicates the group is up.
	Group Stopping: Indicates the group is stopping.
	Group Stopped: Indicates the group is stopped.
	Group Failure: Indicates the group has failed to start.
	Group Disabled: Indicates the group is disabled.(gray)
	Group Enabled: Indicates the group is enabled
	Object Starting: Indicates an object is starting
	Object Stopping: Indicates an object is stopping
	Java Object: Indicates a java process
	Java Object Started: Indicates the java process is up (green)
	Java Object Stopped: Indicates the java process is stopped (red)

Icon	Function
	Java Object Failure: Indicates the java process has failed to start
	Java Object Disabled: Indicates the java object is disabled (gray)
	Process Object: Indicates a process
	Process Object Started: Indicates the process is up (green)
	Process Object Stopped: Indicates the process is stopped (red)
	Process Object Failure: Indicates the process has failed to start
	Process Object Disabled: Indicates the process object is disabled (gray)
	Python Daemon Object: Indicates a python daemon process
	Python Daemon Started: Indicates the python daemon process is up (green)
	Python Daemon Stopped: Indicates the python daemon process is stopped (red)
	Python Daemon Failure: Indicates the python daemon process has failed to start
	Python Daemon Disabled: Indicates the python daemon object is disabled
	Script Object: Indicates a script object

Icon	Function
	Script Object Disabled: Indicates the script object is disabled (gray)
	Script Process Object: Indicates a script process object
	Script Process Started: Indicates the process started by the script is up (green)
	Script Process Stopped: Indicates the process started by the script is stopped (red)
	Script Process Failure: Indicates the process has failed to start
	Script Process Disabled: Indicates the script process object is disabled (gray)
	NXTera Object: Indicates a NXTera object
	NXTera Object Started: Indicates the NXTera process is up (green)
	NXTera Object Stopped: Indicates the NXTera process is stopped (red)
	NXTera Object Failure: Indicates the NXTera process has failed to start
	NXTera Object Disabled: Indicates the NXTera object is disabled (gray)
	File Copy Action: Indicates a File Copy triggered by an event (blue)

Icon	Function
	File Copy Action Disabled: Indicates the File Copy Action object is disabled (gray)
	FTP Action: Indicates a FTP put triggered by an event
	FTP Action Disabled: Indicates the FTP Action object is disabled (gray)
	Mail Action: Indicates a mail send triggered by an event (blue)
	Mail Action Disabled: Indicates the Mail Action object is disabled (gray)
	Script Action: Indicates a script being launched triggered by an event (blue)
	Script Action Disabled: Indicates the Script Action object is disabled (gray)
	Start Timer: Indicates a Start Timer (green)
	Stop Timer: Indicates a Stop Timer (red)
	Timer Disabled: Indicates the Timer object is disabled (gray)
	Unknown: Indicates the object is in some unknown state

The right side of the main panel is the content frame that contains multiple tabs to display specific configuration setting or information about the managed object selected. This frame's contents are determined by the navigation panel selection: highlighting of a configuration, object or action. The content frame can be modified by the authorized NXTmonitor administrator. Samples of the content of these frames are explained below:

Database

The system configuration files for NXTmonitor are stored in an XML-based database that co-exists with the Master Server. The Master Server reads and updates the database when changes occur. Previous versions used a database based on Derby, but current versions use XML. It can be custom-ized to use other SQL92 compliant relational databases like MySQL, Ora-cle, Sybase, DB2 and Informix just to name a few.

NXTmonitor Components Diagram

In diagram below, the three main components of NXTmonitor are shown: the Console, the Agent and the Master Server

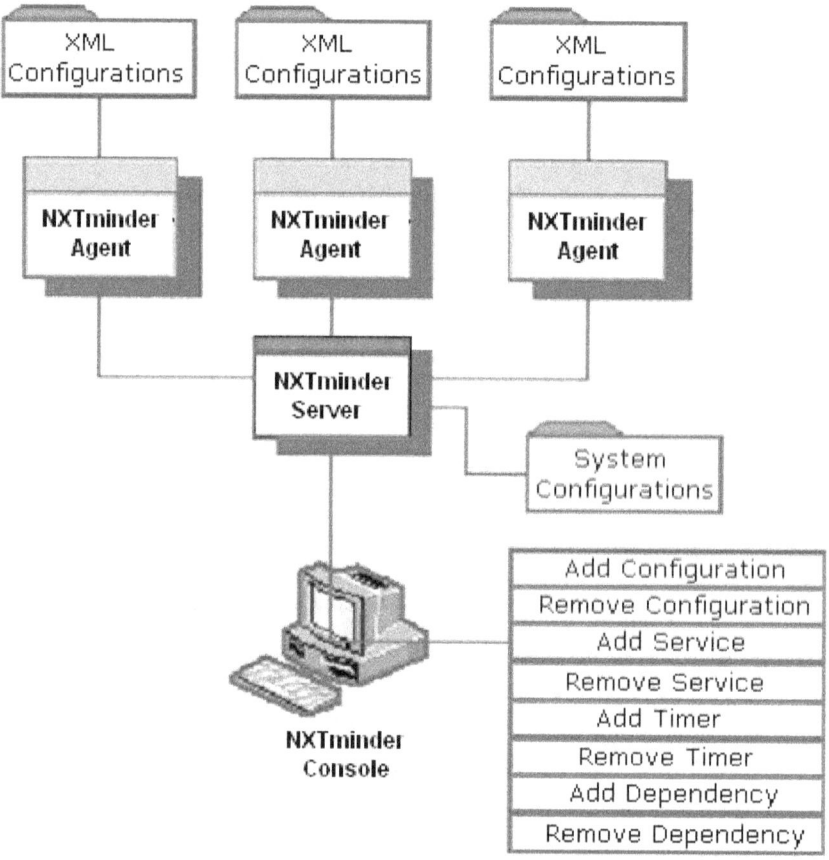

Chapter 3 Starting
NXTmonitor

This section explains how to start up the NXTmonitor in all of its different modes -GUI, TTY, as a server, with security, with the -soft option and more..

Environment Variables (Entera/NXTera)

For Entera and NXTera, the following environment variables need to be set up:

Setting the ODEDIR and PATH environment variables

The ODEDIR and PATH environment variables must be set explicitly, to reflect the location in which Entera utilities are installed. For Entera/TCP and NXTera, ODEDIR must point to the tcp subdirectory below the eCube installation directory. This example shows the syntax for the Bourne shell:

```
ODEDIR=/usr/nxtera/tcp
PATH=$ODEDIR/bin:$PATH
export ODEDIR PATH
```

Setting the ODEDIR and PATH variables is important, because NXTmonitor looks for its executable files in the $ODEDIR/bin directory.

In the Windows 7, 10 and 200X environments, use the System applet in the Control panel to set these environment variables.

Installation

The installation process for NXTmonitor is very simple since it is a Java based application monitoring system. As such, it can be installed on virtually any computer architecture that supports a Java JVM. The installation of NXTmonitor will prompt you for the location of where to put the NXTmonitor installation. Note the directories in which it is installed. You may be prompted for them at a later time.

Requirements:

- NXTmonitor requires Java 1.6 JDK to be installed
- 60 Meg of disk space
- 1 gig of memory

The NXTmonitor software is delivered via ftp or on CD/DVD. To install, copy the zip file to your installation platform and unzip. The zip file will contain three files:

- NXTmonitor_install.jar
- NXTmonitor Users Guide.doc
- NXTmonitor Release notes.txt

The only requirement in Java is that the NXTmonitor Console requires Java 1.6 to be installed. If Java 1.6 is not supported on your target architecture, contact our Technical Support at support@ecubesystems.com to see if you can get earlier version support. The installation software is a stand-alone application specifically written by eCube to be platform independent. The installer can be downloaded from our website or run from the NXTmonitor installation CD/DVD.

Here is a listing of the contents of the zip file with the NXTmonitor soft-ware:

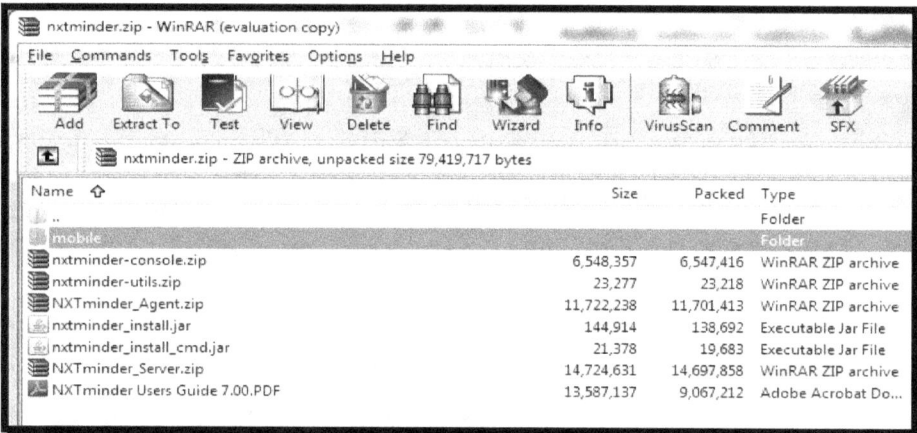

First, extract the zip file to the target directory

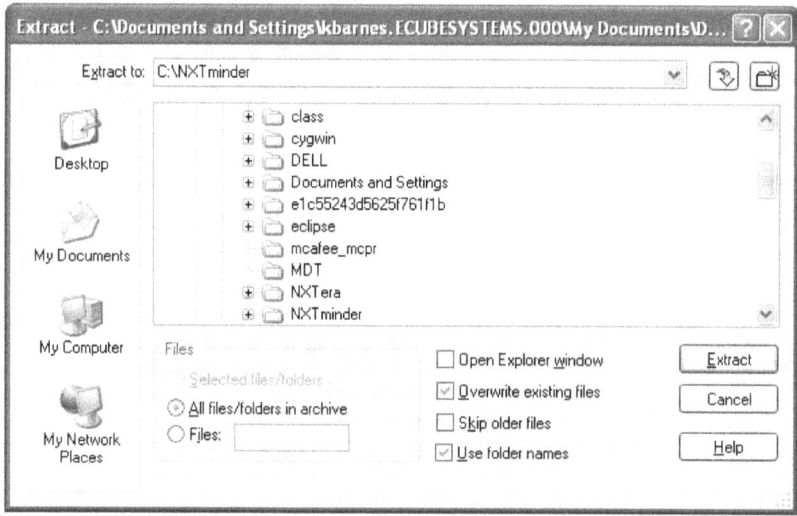

To start the installation process, look at the following platforms below to find the appropriate installation process:

Getting started with Windows

To install the NXTmonitor component on Windows, follow this process:

1. Make sure Java 1.6 is in your path.

2. Bring up a Windows explorer and go to the folder where the installa-tion software was extracted.

3. Double-click the **NXTmonitor_install.jar**.

NOTE: Make sure the .jar file is opened with Java. Or you can run it from the command line with the command:

java -jar NXTmonitor_install.jar

Getting started with UNIX

Follow these steps for installing on a UNIX platform:

1. Make sure you are running these commands from the appropriate userid as all the files will be owned by that user. This user must have permissions to create and start the processes that will be managed.

2. Make sure Java JDK 1.6 is in your path.

3. Change Directory to the directory that contains the **nxtminder_install.jar** or **NXTmonitor_install_cmd.jar**.

4. Run the following command:

java -jar NXTmonitor_install.jar for the GUI version of the installer or **java -jar nxtmonitor_install_cmd.jar** for the command line ver-sion.

Getting started with MacOS

From the directory that contains the **nxtmonitor_install.jar** you can either double-click the icon on the file manager window or run the following command in a terminal window:

    java -jar nxtmonitor_install.jar

The notes from the UNIX installation also apply to Mac OS.

The installation application will launch the following screen to prompt the user for the installation options. Based on the available systems chosen in the System Requirements section, the user installs each of the three compo-nents: Server, Agent and Console. On the following pages, the installation screens and selections are listed for each of the three components. Follow the step by step instructions for each.

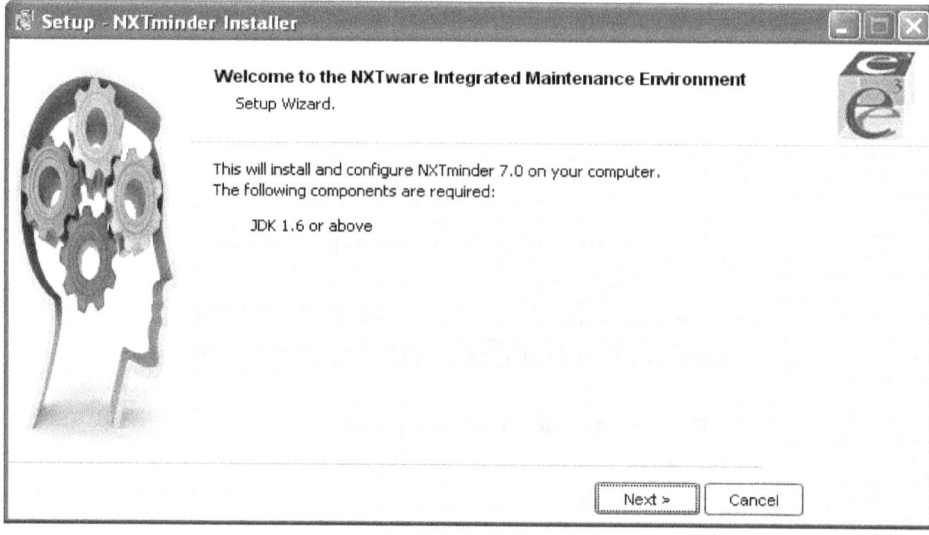

IMPORTANT NOTE: <u>Make sure you follow the installation component order</u>; the server first, then the agent, and then the console. This is important because the server IP address is used in the Agent install process, so it will either have to be installed first, or the IP needs to be known.

A command line installer is available for the master server and agents components. You can run the command line installer with the following command:

java -jar nxtmonitor_install_cmd.jar

If you are using the command line installer, you will need to use the Administration tool to enter the license information and the license file. Check the **License Manager** section for more details.

Server Installation

The Master Server installation can be performed by running the **nxtmonitor_install.jar** on the target machine. The following screen should appear:

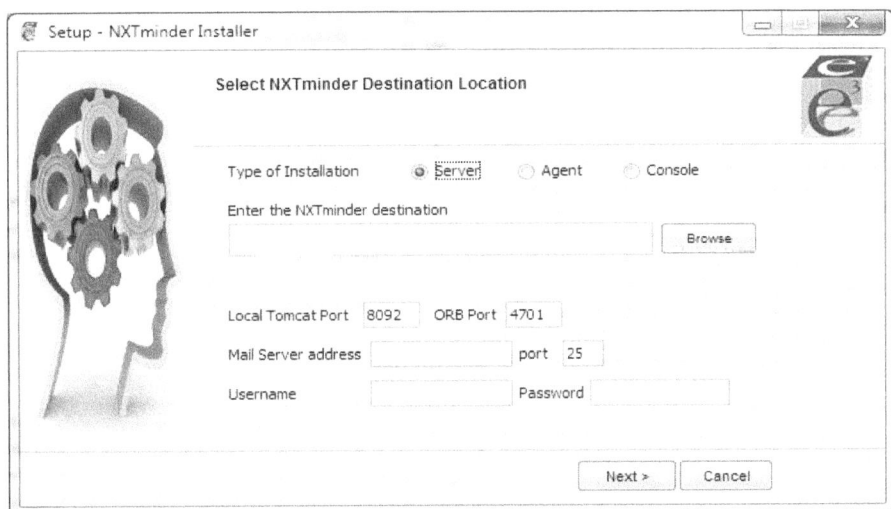

1. Enter the destination directory of the NXTmonitor server. (please note this for future reference)

2. If you intend to create Mail Action objects, provide the address of the mail server and the port number if different than 25. Enter a user-name and a password if necessary.

3. NXTmonitor uses two ports. You can change the default ports. If using a firewall and if you intend to monitor the system from the out-side, make sure the two ports are accessible.

4. Click the **Next** button.

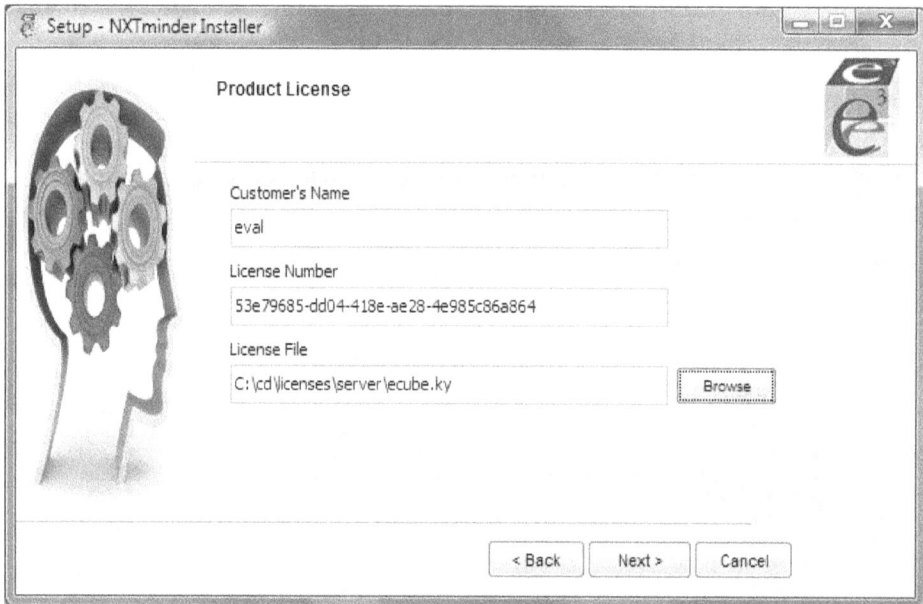

5. Fill the product license information.

6. Click the **Next** button. On the next screen, click the **Install** button.

To Start the Server:

- On Windows: run **start-server.bat** that can be found in the **<Installed Directory>/NXTmonitor_Server/bin**

- On Unix or MacOS: run **start-server.sh** that can be found in the **<Installed Directory>/NXTmonitor_Server/bin**

The server component is the agent's central repository. The server component includes an agent. You will install agents on different machines that you wish to monitor through the master server (agent's central repository).

Agent Installation

The Agent installation is also performed by running the **nxtmonitor_install.jar** on the target machine. The following screen should appear:

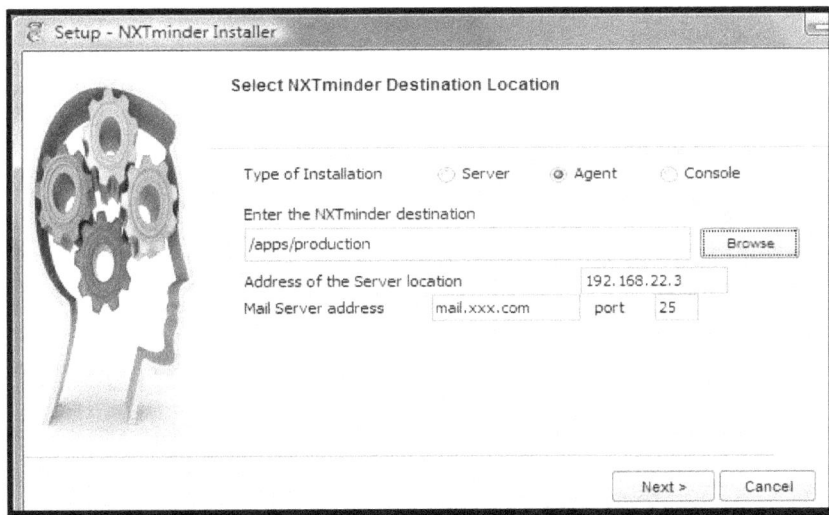

NOTE: Agent will not run on the same machine as a Server if it is running because Server includes an Agent. Do not install Agent on a computer that already has Server installed.

1. Enter the destination directory of the NXTmonitor agent.

2. Enter the IP address or server name of the master server (**see Server Installation**).

3. If you intend to create Mail Action objects, provide the address of the mail server and the port number if different than 25. Enter a username and a password if necessary.

4. NXTmonitor uses two ports. You can change the default ports. If using a firewall and if you intend to monitor the system from the outside, make sure the two ports are accessible. The ORB Port must be the same as the ORB Port on the master server.

5. Click the **Next** button.

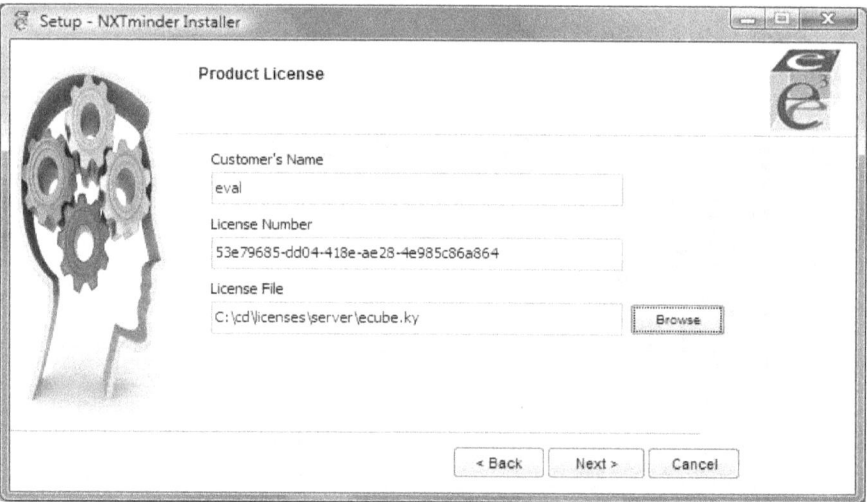

6. Fill the product license information.

7. Click the **Next** button. On the next screen, click the **Install** button.

To start the agent:

- On Windows: run **start-agent.bat** that can be found in the **<Installed Directory>/NXTmonitor_Agent/bin**

- On Unix or MacOS: run **start-agent.sh** that can be found in the **<Installed Directory>/NXTmonitor_Agent/bin**

Console Installation

The Console installation is also performed by running the nxtmonitor_install.jar on the target machine. If there is more than one com-puter you wish to run the NXTmonitor Console on, you can ftp the installer and the console zip file to the other machines. Once on the target machine, you can start the java installer process. The following screen should appear:

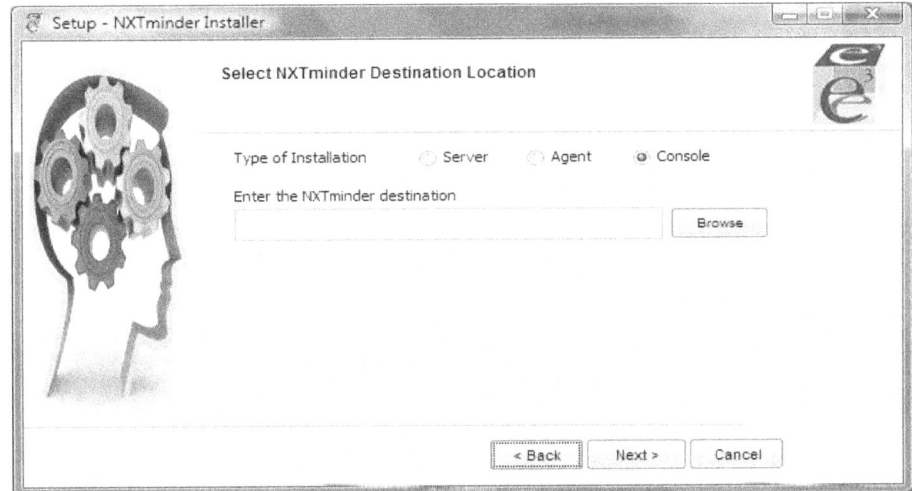

1. Enter the destination directory of the NXTmonitor console.

2. Click the **Next** button and the **Install** button.

3. To start the console, run **nxtmonitor-console.bat** that can be found in the **<Installed Directory>/nxtmonitor-console** or click on the desktop icon.

Security

Once the console is installed, the default usernames and passwords provided in this manual should be changed. For this reason, NXTmonitor provides a Web interface for the management of users. For more information, see the next chapter on NXTmonitor Administration.

NXTmonitor Startup

Running NXTmonitor

This section contains information on using NXTmonitor to start managing and monitoring your applications. Before you start the console which is the visual component of NXTmonitor you should start the services first.

Getting Started with Licenses

To start managing your applications, you should start the NXTmonitor Master Server and any applicable Agent services first. Before doing that, you need to copy your license into the applicable license directories before pro-ceeding. You will get a default 60 day evaluation license with the NXTmonitor install; it may be expired and you will need to obtain a new license.

To obtain a new license, email support@ecubesystems.com and we will email you a new evaluation license. If you have purchased NXTera with NXTmonitor, you will get a product license emailed to the registered email address with the NXTera license. To install the license, do the following:

1. A file named license.xml contains the NXTmonitor license and it has to be copied into the Server, Agent and Console license directories.

2. Either copy and paste the license.xml file into the appropriate direc-tories or:

3. Run:

copy license.xml <NXTmonitor-install- directory>/NXTmonitor_Server/license copy

license.xml <NXTmonitor install directory>/NXTmonitor_Agent/license copy

license.xml <NXTmonitor install directory>/NXTmonitor_Console/license

Starting the Server

To start the Server, issue the start-server command in a command line prompt

- `cd <NXTmonitor install directory>/NXTmonitor_Server/ bin`
- `start-server`

If you have a valid license file, the NXTmonitor server will start services. You should get the following messages in a command window:

Starting the Agent

To start the Agent, issue the start-agent command in a command line prompt.

- `cd <NXTmonitor install directory>/NXTmonitor_Agent/bin`
- `start-agent`

If you have a valid license file, the NXTmonitor Agent will start services. You should get the following messages in a command window:

Starting the Console

Once the Server and Agent(s) (on other computers) have been started, the NXTmonitor Console can then be started. To start the Agent, issue the start-console.bat command in a command line prompt on Windows **(or you can double-click on the bat file in an explorer window)**:

- `cd <NXTmonitor install directory>/NXTmonitor_Console/bin`
- `start-console.bat`

If you have a valid license file, the NXTmonitor Console will launch and will begin logging to a log file. A command window will appear along with this window:

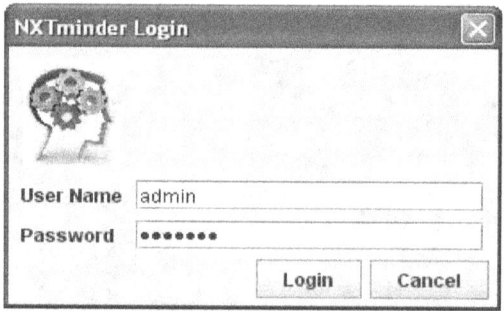

Once you log in with default user: **admin** and password: **nxtware**. The Console GUI will appear with an empty configuration in the navigation window:

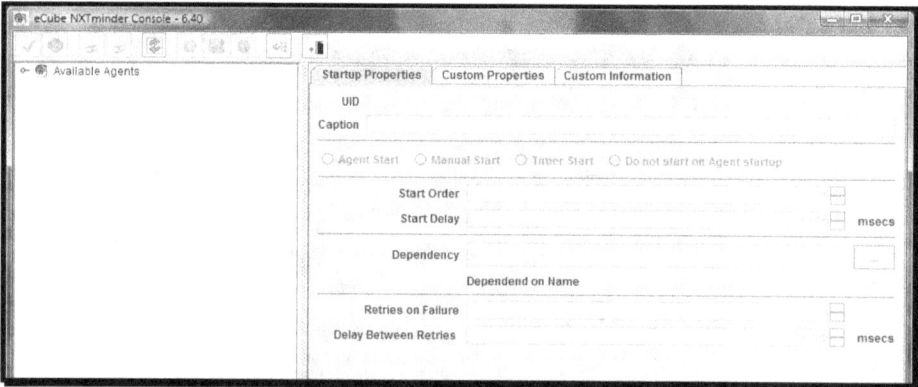

To view available agents, open the folder "Available Agents" and the host-name of your running Agents and the Main Group underneath it will appear:

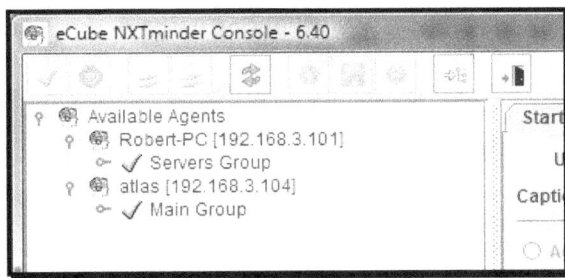

To add servers or groups, select the Main Group and use the action buttons at the top of the GUI to add, remove, start and stop servers or groups to this agent's configuration. (see **"Action Icons"** of the Architecture section in Chapter 4 for button explanations). If multiple agents are started, their con-figurations will also appear in the NXTmonitor Console. To perform these actions consult the section on Action buttons for the appropriate icon to choose. The NXTmonitor Console also generates a log file which is nor-mally empty.**Scripts notes:**

- On Windows, start-server or start-agent will reference to **start-server.bat** and **start-agent.bat**

- On Unix, start-server or start-agent will reference to **start-server.sh** and **start-agent.sh**.

Adding Master Agents

The console allows you to monitor multiple master agents at once. Each master agent can have one or more agent node attach to.

To add a master agent:

1. Select the Master Agents tree node.

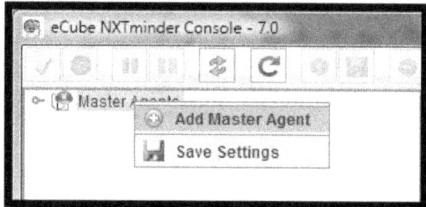

2. Right-click and select **Add Master Agent**.

3. Fill the information:

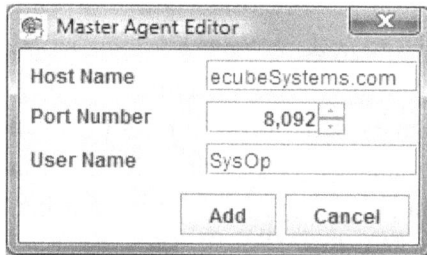

Host Name is the name or IP address of the master server.

Port Number is the Tomcat port of the master server.

User Name is a valid admin or operator user.

4. Save your settings.

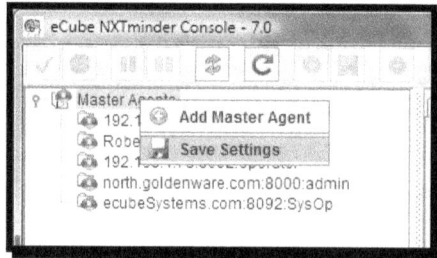

Connecting to a Master Agent

To connect to a master server:

1. Select the master agent node and right-click.

2. Select the **Connect** option.

3. Enter the username and password.

Editing a Connection

To edit a master server connection:

1. Select the master agent node and right-click.

2. Select the **Edit Connection** option.

3. Make your changes.

4. Select the **Master Agents** node.

5. Right-click and select the **Save Settings** option.

Deleting a Connection

To delete a master server connection:

1. Select the master agent node and right-click.

2. Select the **Delete** option.

3. Select the **Master Agents** node.

4. Right-click and select the **Save Settings** option.

Stopping the Console

You stop or exit the Console clicking the exit button. Exiting the console will not affect the management of the servers; it only stops the GUI. The managed servers/objects will remain under management.

Stopping the Agent and Server

If you need to stop the Server and Agent(s) after they have been started, the best way to do that is to Control-C the services within the command window.

cd <NXTmonitor install directory>/NXTmonitor_Console/

bin Ctrl+C

Terminate batch job(Y/N)?   Y

This chapter covers the NXTmonitor infrastructure, so that the user is more familiar with it.

Don't forget to start a NXTmonitor agent on every host where NXTmonitor will be monitoring services! Nothing will work if a agent is not running.

NXTmonitor Administration

This section outlines the administration tasks associated with NXTmonitor. Step by step instructions are given to demonstrate the creation and maintainance of user accounts within NXTmonitor as well as maintenance tasks.

Users NXTmonitor Console access is managed with a Username and Password interface. In order to access the master agent, you will have to login and supply the required credentials. Additional users can be added with the Administration interface located within the Master Server.

The interface uses an administrator user name and password to log in. The admin interface uses a default user name: **admin**, Password for admin is **nxtware**. To use the administration web interface, type the following into your browser line:

http://<your IP Address>:<tomcat port>/admin (login with admin username)

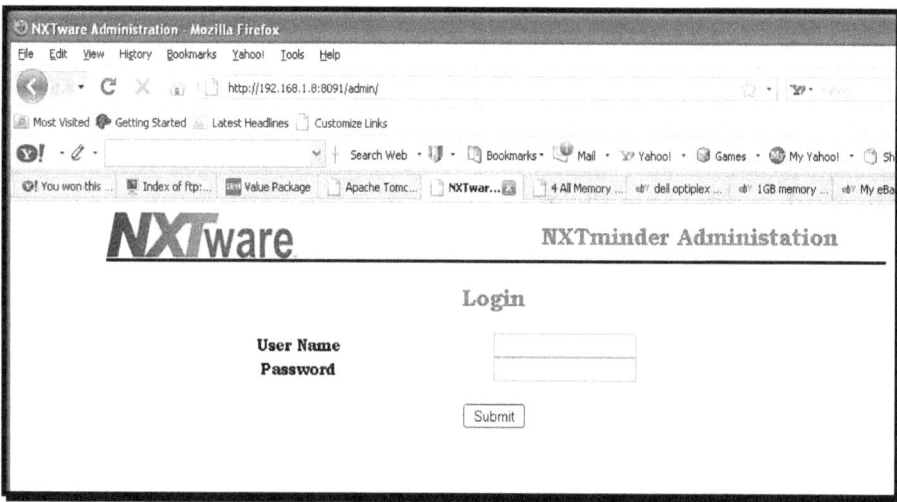

That will launch the administration interface below:

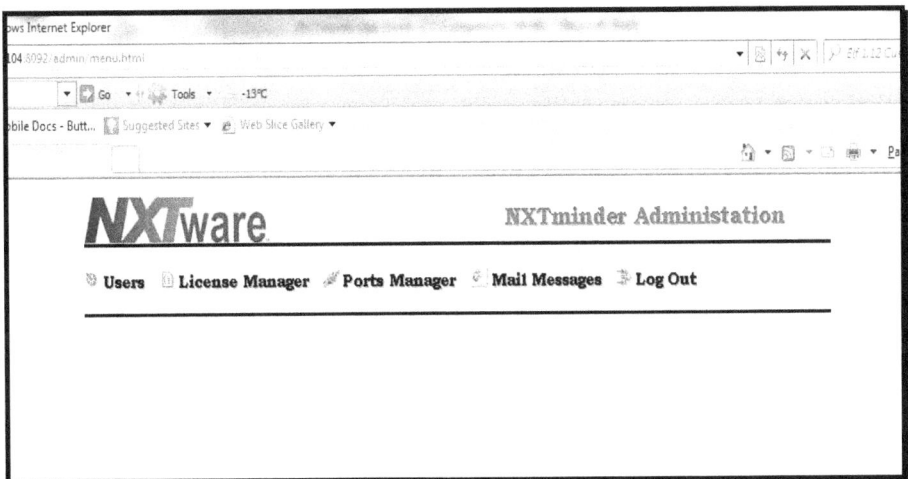

Select **Users** and use the links provided to add, edit or delete a user for NXTmonitor.

Creating users

Creating users is the main function of the Administrator interface.

There are two types of users.

- **Administrator:** can create, edit, and delete configurations, objects and managed them.

- **Operator:** can only start and stop configurations or objects.

To create a new user, click on the **"add a new user"** field. It should bring up the following screen:

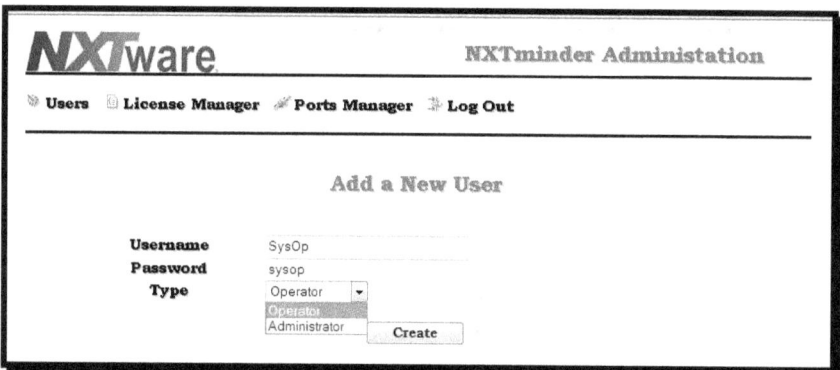

Choose a unique user name with a password and the type of console user privilege for this user. Once the operator user has been added, you can start NXTmonitor console and enter the username and password. The login window is shown below:

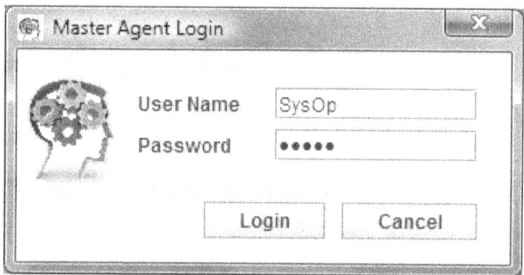

Edit a user's entry

Presently, only an administrator can edit the user entry and the only function available is to change a user's password.

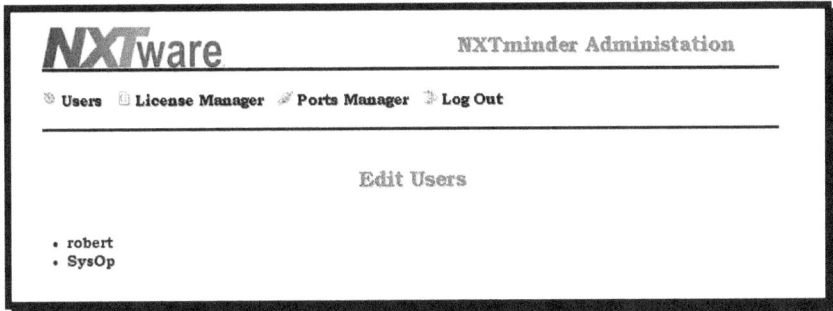

Select the desired user. You can only modify the password.

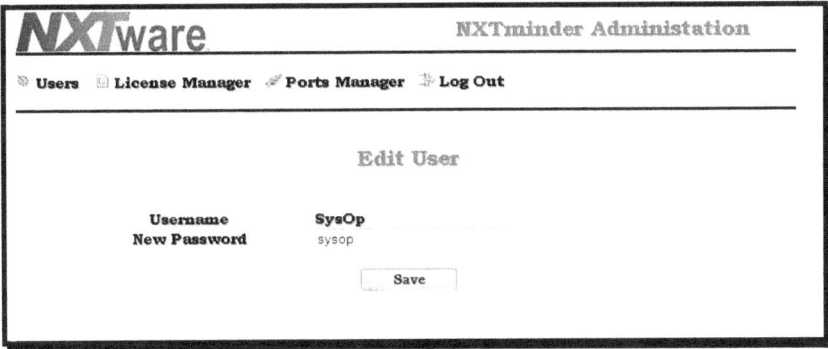

Deleting a User

The Administrator interface also allows you to delete a user by selecting **Delete a User**. Click on the user that you want to delete and confirm. The following box should appear asking for confirmation.

As indicated, click on OK to delete or Cancel to cancel deletion of this user.

License Manager

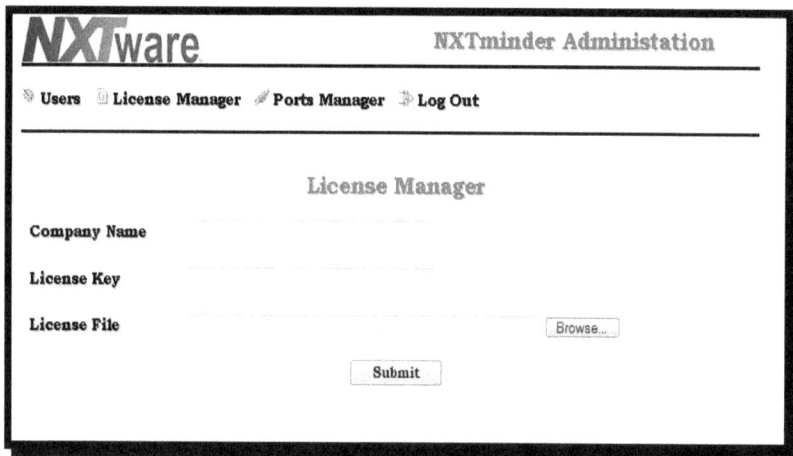

The License Manager section allows you to add or update the server license. This option is also available for the agent.

Ports Manager

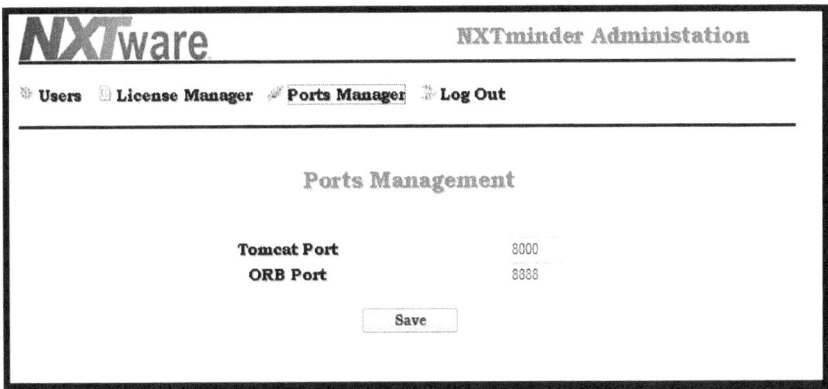

The Ports Manager section allows you to modify the server's listening port. This option is also available for the agent.

All the agents registered with a master server should all have the same ORB Port.

You will need to restart the server and/or the agent(s) in order for these changes to take effect.

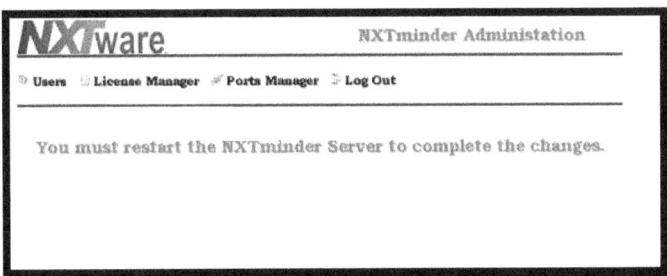

Mail Messages

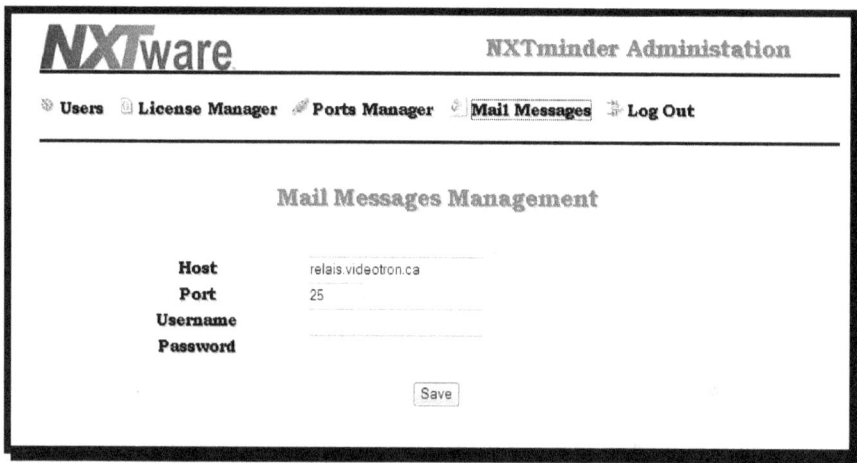

The Mail Messages Management section allows you to modify the mail server properties. This option is also available for the agent.

You will need to restart the server and/or the agent(s) in order for these changes to take effect.

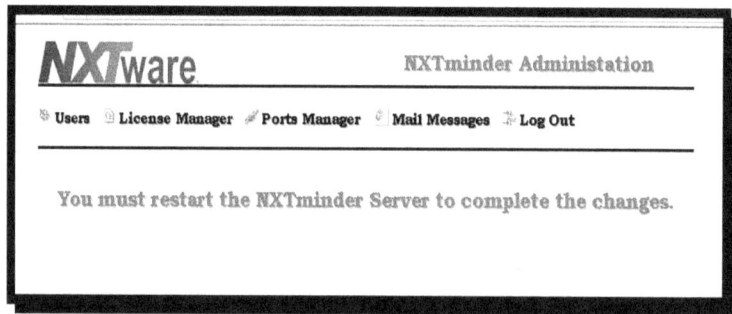

Managing Applications

This chapter contains information on how to manage distributed applications using the NXTmonitor tools. The NXTmonitor configuration files will be introduced and step by step instructions on how to set up management options for different types of managed objects will be provided.

Configurations

Using Configurations, NXTmonitor enables you to group and manage distributed resources. NXTmonitor enables you to control, monitor and manage these resources as a single entity.

Each agent configuration is stored in an AgentSetup.xml file. Agents are looking for the **AgentSetup.xml** file. It is important that you do not rename any of the xml or dtd files.

Performance

In using NXTmonitor Console, be aware that all of the configuration files you are modifying with the GUI are maintained in a database on the Master Server. As such, there will be a delay in updating the screen when you make changes. This is done to ensure the changes are transmitted to the database and the update was successful. If the performance of these tasks is too slow, you can modify the MonitoringClient properties file and reduce the number of seconds. The default is set to 30 seconds and it can be reduced as low as 10 seconds without significant harmful network traffic. Contents of MonitoringClient.properties file:

- `com.monitoring.client.main.readURL=http://192.168.1.8:8091/CorbaFederationsServlet?action=read&federationName=MonitoringAgentFederation`
- `com.monitoring.client.main.refreshInterval=30000`

NOTE: Reducing the Monitoring Client properties value below 10 seconds, could cause NXTmonitor to send out excessive network packets and could impact network performance. Consult your network engineer before attempting this.

Dependencies

Often it is necessary to have one object rely on another due to some software service or component dependency. Suppose one of the objects in your application connects to a naming service upon start-up (such as the dependency of NXTera servers upon the Broker). In this case, the naming service needs to be up and running prior to the starting of your objects. This is a *dependency*; specifically a *start dependency*.

Dependencies are a way of further defining your distributed application's behavior in NXTmonitor. Dependencies can exist between:

- Managed objects
- Groups
- Groups and Managed objects

Grouping objects means that there is an implicit dependency shared by members of that group.

Start Order

Where a group contains numerous objects or services, another way to decide the startup order is to use the Start Order property in the object's Startup properties. Weighting allows you specify which objects NXTmonitor will try to start up first by assigning a weighting number to them.Objects with a lower number are started first.

Fault Tolerance

Fault tolerance is the ability of your application to survive the failure of one or more components in the distributed application. If one component in your application fails, you still want your application to continue running if it can. This can be accomplished through the use of the fault-tolerant relationship.

The fault-tolerant relationship specifies a backup relationship between two objects that generally perform the same functionality. If one object fails, the next object is brought up to replace the failed object. Your middleware is then responsible for diverting calls to the backup object in order to maintain the integrity of your application.

In this way, your application does not fail when one object in your application is unavailable. The switch from one object to the next is performed seamlessly and is transparent to the user.

Defining Failover

Failover is an action that lets you bring up a replacement object or service before bringing down the one being replaced. The new object is started without any interruption in service to the users. Of course, this assumes that there is no new procedure necessary to make the client compatible with the new object. For more information, see "Warnings about fault tolerance and load balancing".

Defining Load Balancing

Load Balancing is the ability to evenly spread the client calls in your distributed application across a number of objects or servers that perform the same function. Theoretically, there are two ways that once can accomplish load balancing: dynamically and statically.

Managed Objects

You use the Management Console to create and add new Managed Objects to your Configurations. Managed objects are stored as entries in the NXTmonitor database and can either be Groups, Events, Timers or Servers.

You use the Management Console to create and add new Managed Objects to your Configurations. Managed objects are stored as entries in the NXTmonitor database and can either be Groups, Events, Timers or Launchers. The following section documents what groups are and how they are used by NXTmonitor.

Master Groups

 A Master Group is used to define a configuration. A Master Group can have Events, Timers and Launchers. It can be dependent of another Master Group or another object within another Master Group.

Create a Master Group

In order to create a Master Group, you must select the agent node. Once you have highlighted this in the navigation panel, right-click and select **Add Master Group**. Here is an example of the options if you right-click on a **Master Group**:

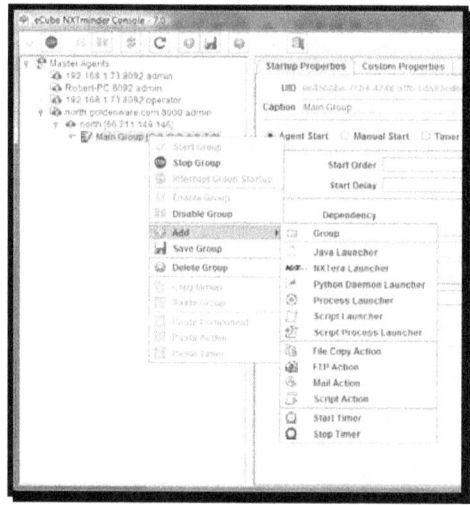

Delete a Master Group

If you want to delete a Master Group, click on the group name in the navigation window and click on the **Delete** toolbar button. The following pop-up window should appear:

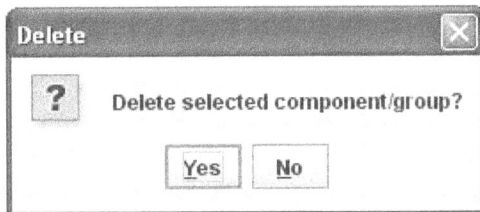

Renaming a Master Group

To rename a **Master Group**, click on the Master Group name in the navigation panel. In the content panel, change the name in the caption box under Startup Properties and click on the **Save** toolbar button.

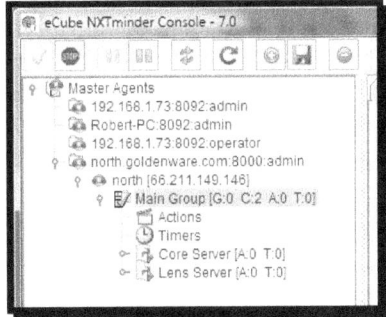

Startup Properties

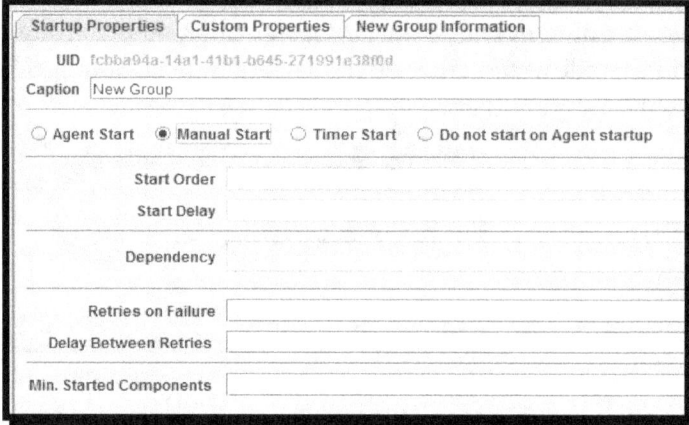

Startup Options:

- **Agent Start:** the Agent will start and stop the Group.
- **Manual Start:** started from the console by clicking the start button.
- **Timer Start:** started by a Start Timer Object.

Start Order: objects with lower numbers are started first within the Group they belong. You might want to have a higher number than an object that the Group is dependent on.

Start Delay: how long should the group wait to start after the start event is triggered?

Dependency: attach a start and stop dependency based on the status of another object. For example, if the objects inside the Master Group require that a Naming Service is up and running, the Group will start and stop based on the status of the Naming Service.

Retries on Failure: number of times the agent will try to start the Group before marking it as having FAILED.

Delay between Retries: time in milliseconds between retries.

Groups

A Group is a way in NXTmonitor to define another set of objects that can be treated as an entity to receive the same commands in one operation. You use a Group to identify a collection of Managed Objects within a Configu-ration for the following purposes:

- To define the order that NXTmonitor will use to start and stop the Managed Objects within the context of the Group or the Configuration.

- To add a dependency to another Managed Object to the Group.

Create a Group

In order to create a Group, you must select the Master Group or another Group. Once you have highlighted this in the navigation panel, click on the **Add** toolbar button to add the Group to the Master Group. Here is an example of the options if you right click on a Group:

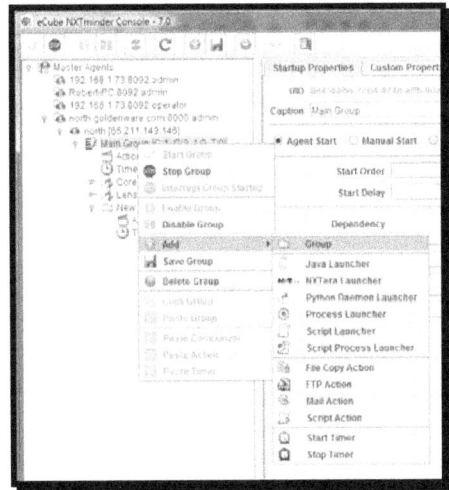

Delete a Group

If you want to delete a Group, click on the group name in the navigation window and click on the **Delete** toolbar button. The following pop-up window should appear:

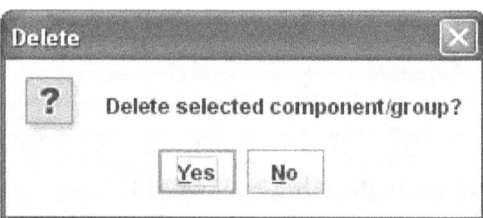

Renaming a Group

To rename a Group, click on the Group name in the navigation panel. In the content panel, change the name in the caption box under Startup Properties and click the **Save** toolbar button.

Startup Properties

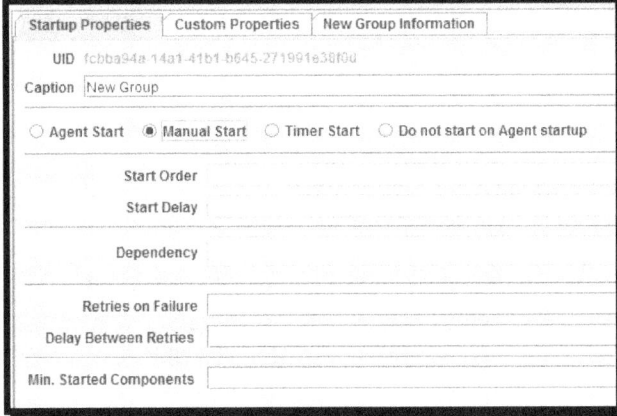

Startup Options:

- **Agent Start:** the Agent will start and stop the Group.
- **Manual Start:** started from the console by clicking the start button.
- **Timer Start:** started by a Start Timer Object.

Start Order: objects with lower numbers are started first within the Group they belong. You might want to have a higher number than an object that the Group is dependent on.

Start Delay: how long should the group wait to start after the start event is triggered?

Dependency: attach a start and stop dependency based on the status of another object. For example, if the objects inside the Group require that a Naming Service is up and running, the Group will start and stop based on the status of the Naming Service.

Retries on Failure: number of times the agent will try to start the Group before marking it as having FAILED.

Delay between Retries: time in milliseconds between retries.

Launchers

Java Launcher

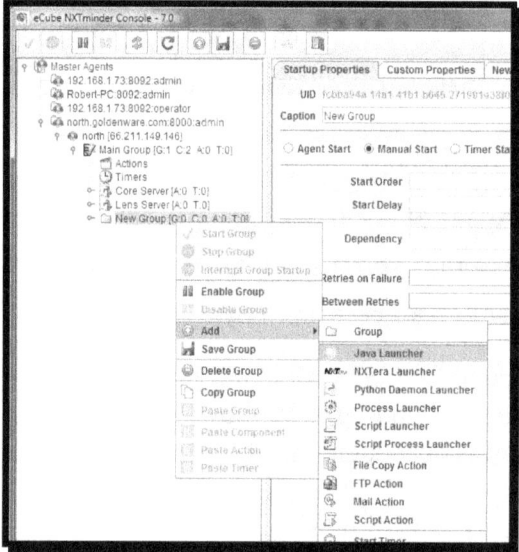 NXTmonitor has a Java Launcher Object you can use to start a Java Program. This screen shot below shows the menu item under which it is found:

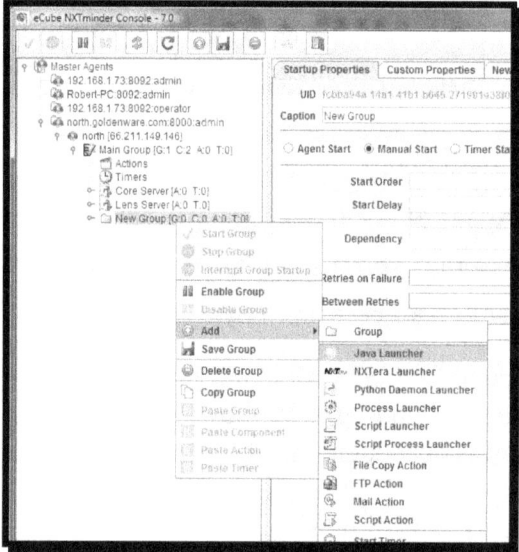

Startup Properties

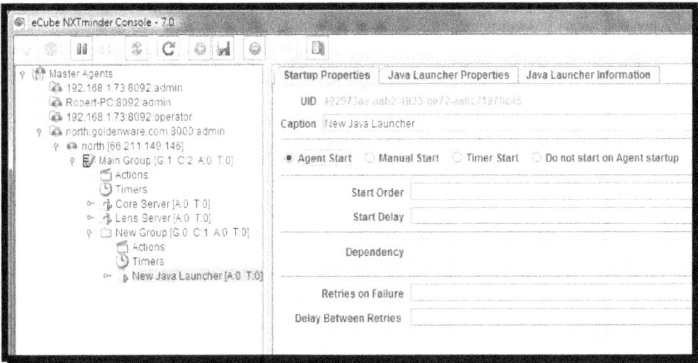

Startup Options:

- **Agent Start:** the Agent will start and stop the Object.
- **Manual Start:** started from the console by clicking the start button.
- **Timer Start:** started by a Start Timer Object.

Start Order: objects with lower numbers are started first within the Group they belong. You might want to have a higher number than an object that this Object is dependent on.

Start Delay: how long should the object wait to start after the start event is triggered?

Dependency: attach a start and stop dependency based on the status of another object. For example, if the object requires that a Naming Service is up and running, the Object will start and stop based on the status of the Naming Service.

Retries on Failure: number of times the agent will try to start the Object before marking it as having FAILED.

Delay between Retries: time in milliseconds between retries.

Java Launcher Properties are: (! indicates a mandatory field)

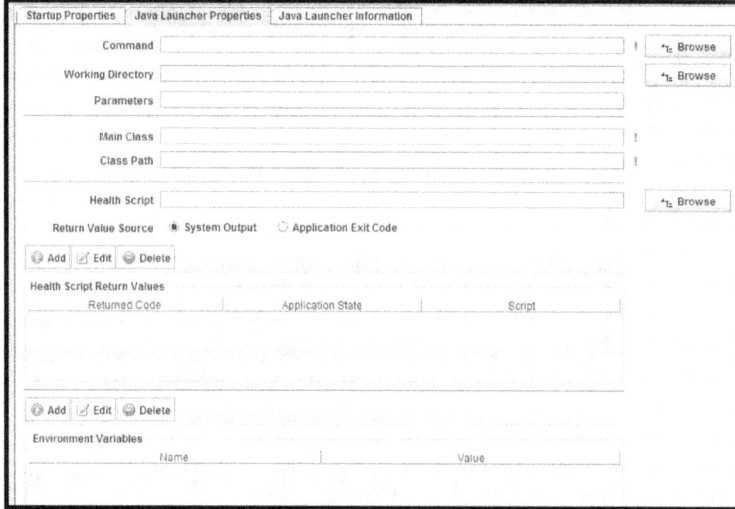

- **! Command:** the command line and the jvm parameters if any.
- **Working Directory:** the working directory.
- **Parameters:** main class parameters.
- **! Main Class:** the java class name.
- **! ClassPath:** the java classpath.

Health Script properties and usage are described in the Health Script section.

You can add, edit or delete System Environment Variables using the **Add**, **Edit**, or **Delete** buttons.

NXTera Launcher

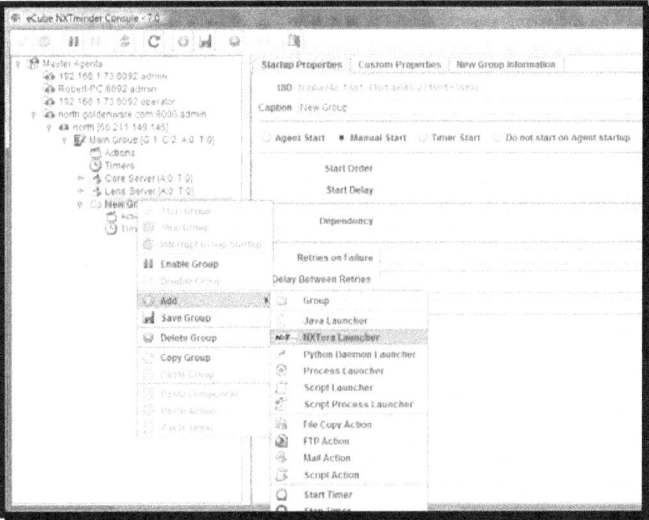 You use an NXTera Launcher Object to start an Entera or NXTera broker or service.

Startup Properties

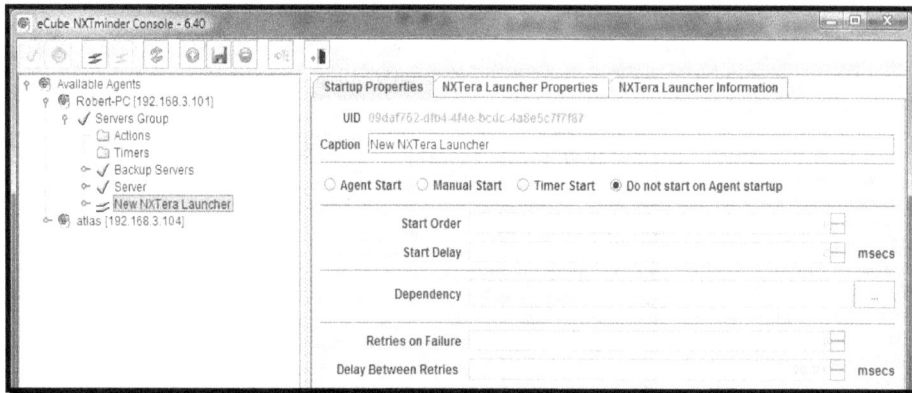

Startup Options:

- **Agent Start:** the Agent will start and stop the Object.
- **Manual Start:** started from the console by clicking the start button.
- **Timer Start:** started by a Start Timer Object.

Start Order: objects with lower numbers are started first within the Group they belong. You might want to have a higher number than an object that this Object is dependent on.

Start Delay: how long should the object wait to start after the start event is triggered?

Dependency: attach a start and stop dependency based on the status of another object. For example, if the object requires that a Naming Service is up and running, the Object will start and stop based on the status of the Naming Service.

Retries on Failure: number of times the agent will try to start the Object before marking it as having FAILED.

Delay between Retries: time in milliseconds between retries.

NXTera Launcher Properties are: (! indicates a mandatory field)

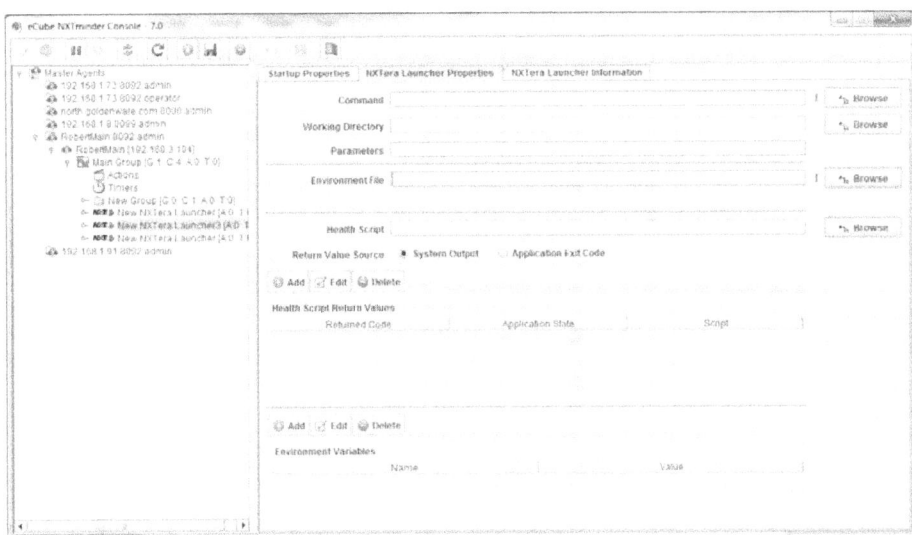

- **! Command:** the command line to execute the application goes here.

- **Working Directory:** the working directory where the application will store its files is entered here.

- **Parameters:** extra command line parameters beside the -e <env-File>.

- **! Environment File:** the Entera or NXTera environment file.

Health Script properties and usage are described in the Health Script section.

You can add, edit or delete System Environment Variables using the **Add**, **Edit**, or **Delete** buttons.

Process Launcher

 You use a Process Launcher to start any executable.

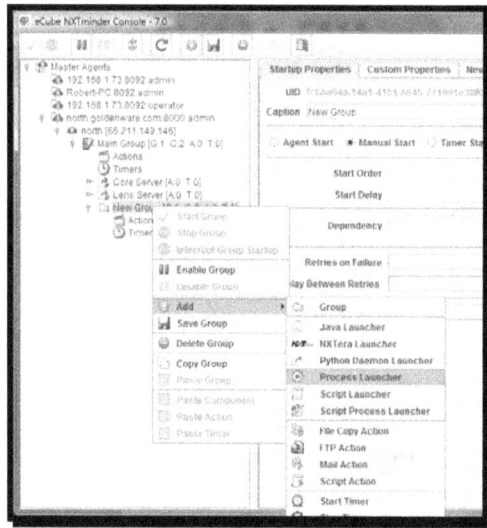

Startup Properties

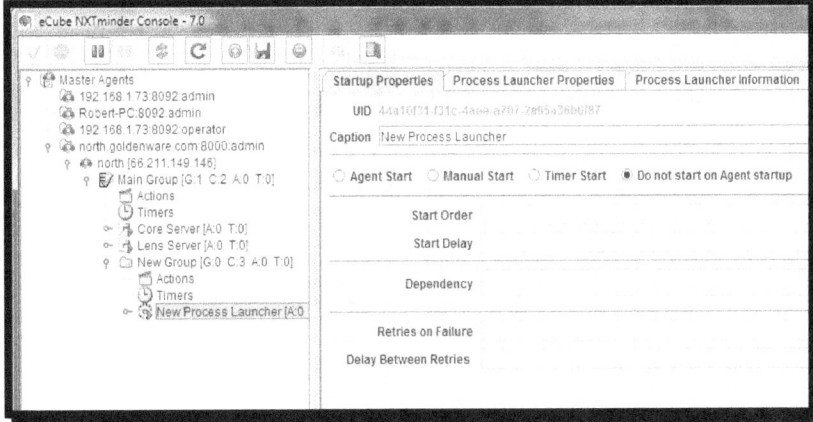

Startup Options:

- **Agent Start:** the Agent will start and stop the Object.
- **Manual Start:** started from the console by clicking the start button.
- **Timer Start:** started by a Start Timer Object.

Start Order: objects with lower numbers are started first within the Group they belong. You might want to have a higher number than an object that this Object is dependent on.

Start Delay: how long should the object wait to start after the start event is triggered?

Dependency: attach a start and stop dependency based on the status of another object. For example, if the object requires that a Naming Service is up and running, the Object will start and stop based on the status of the Naming Service.

Retries on Failure: number of times the agent will try to start the Object before marking it as having FAILED.

Delay between Retries: time in milliseconds between retries.

Process Launcher Properties are: (! indicates a mandatory field)

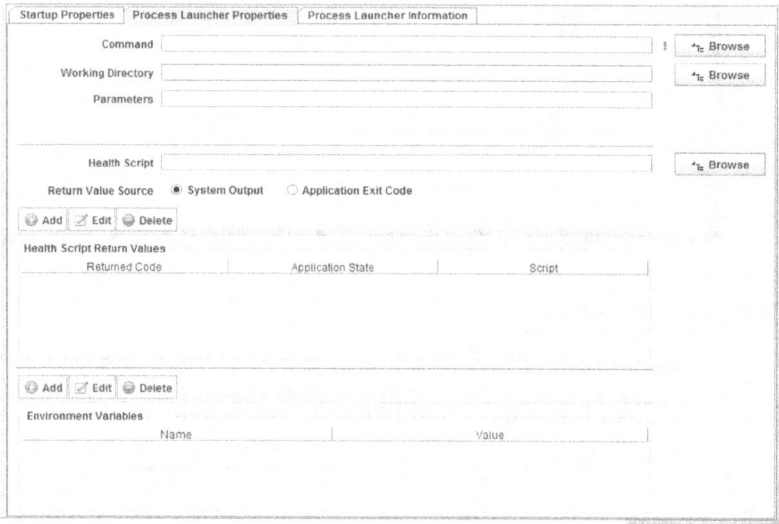

- **! Command:** the command line.
- **Working Directory:** the working directory.
- **Parameters:** command line parameters.

Health Script properties and usage are described in the Health Script section.

You can add, edit or delete System Environment Variables using the **Add**, **Edit**, or **Delete** buttons.

Script Launcher

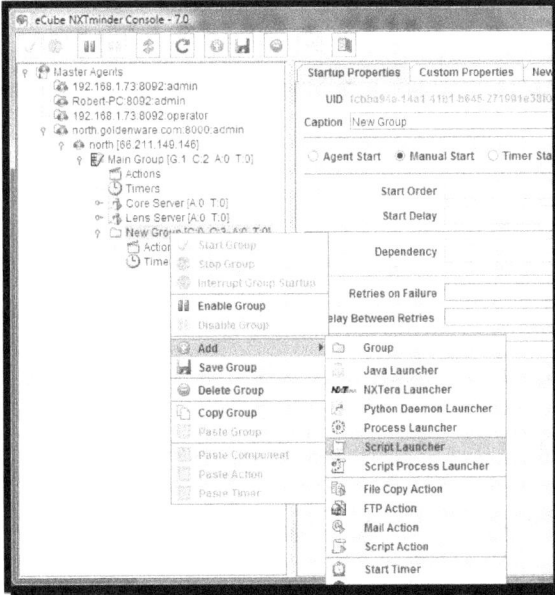 You use a Script Launcher to execute a script, a bat file, or a process that will not be monitored by NXTmonitor.

Startup Properties

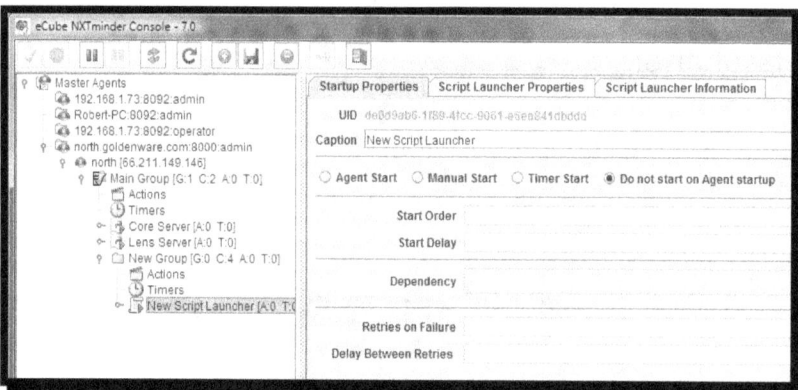

Startup Options:

- **Agent Start:** the Agent will start and stop the Object.
- **Manual Start:** started from the console by clicking the start button.
- **Timer Start:** started by a Start Timer Object.

Start Order: objects are with lower numbers are started first within the Group they belong. You might want to have a higher number than an object that this Object is dependent on.

Start Delay: how long should the object wait to start after the start event is triggered?

Dependency: attach a start and stop dependency based on the status of another object. For example, if the object requires that a Naming Service is up and running, the Object will start and stop based on the status of the Naming Service.

Retries on Failure: number of times the agent will try to start the Object before marking it as having FAILED.

Delay between Retries: time in milliseconds between retries.

Script Launcher Properties are: (! indicates a mandatory field)

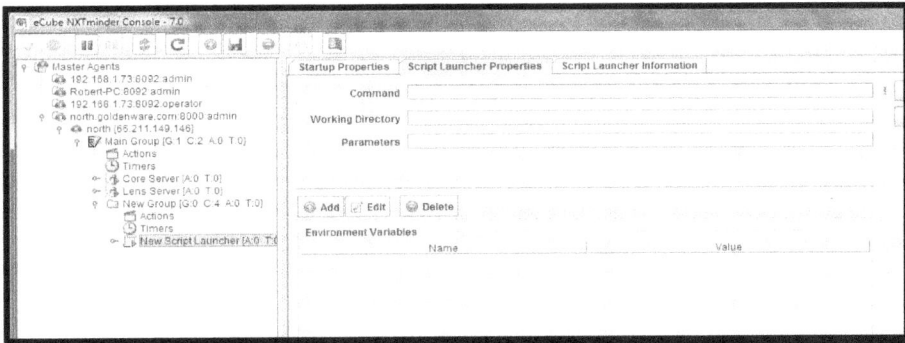

- **! Command:** the command line.
- **Working Directory:** the working directory.
- **Parameters:** command line parameters.

You can add, edit or delete System Environment Variables using the **Add**, **Edit**, or **Delete** buttons.

Script Process Launcher

 You use a Script Process Launcher to start an application using a script or a bat file, and you want NXTmonitor to monitor the application started by the script or the bat file.

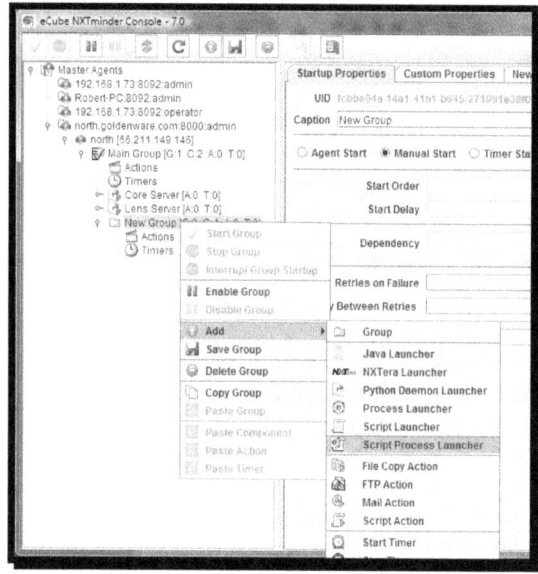

Startup Properties

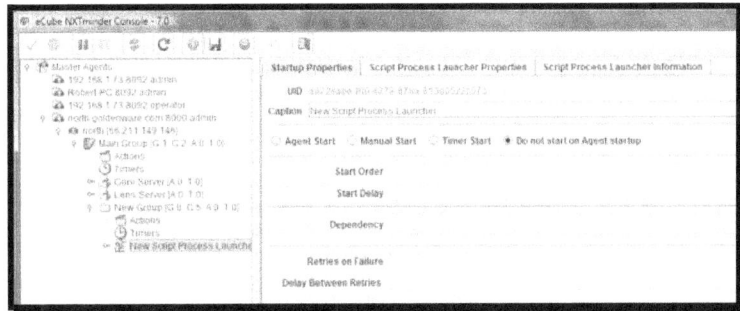

Startup Options:

- **Agent Start:** the Agent will start and stop the Object.
- **Manual Start:** started from the console by clicking the start button.
- **Timer Start:** started by a Start Timer Object.

Start Order: objects are with lower numbers are started first within the Group they belong. You might want to have a higher number than an object that this Object is dependent on.

Start Delay: how long should the object wait to start after the start event is triggered?

Dependency: attach a start and stop dependency based on the status of another object. For example, if the object requires that a Naming Service is up and running, the Object will start and stop based on the status of the Naming Service.

Retries on Failure: number of times the agent will try to start the Object before marking it as having FAILED.

Delay between Retries: time in milliseconds between retries.

Script Process Launcher Properties are: (! indicates a mandatory field)

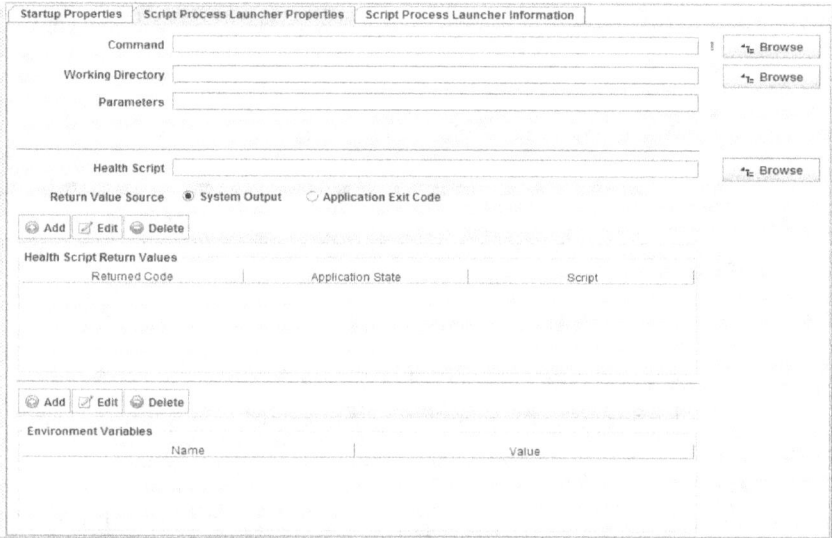

- **! Command:** the command line.
- **Working Directory:** the working directory.
- **Parameters:** command line parameters.

Health Script properties and usage are described in the Health Script section.

You can add, edit or delete System Environment Variables using the **Add**, **Edit**, or **Delete** buttons.

Python Daemon Launcher

 You use a Python Daemon Launcher to start a python server using a script or a bat file, and you want NXTmonitor to monitor the application started by the script or the bat file. The server must store the process identifier in a file.

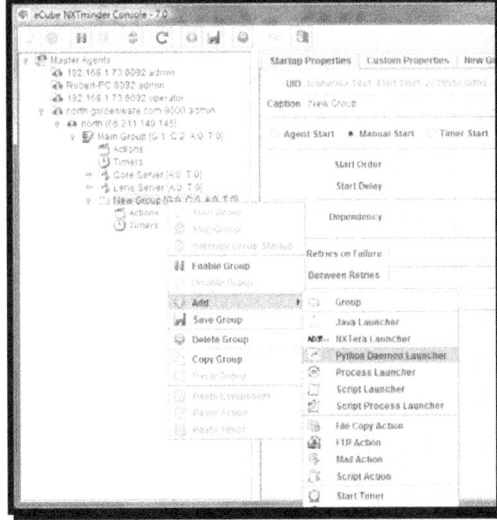

Startup Properties

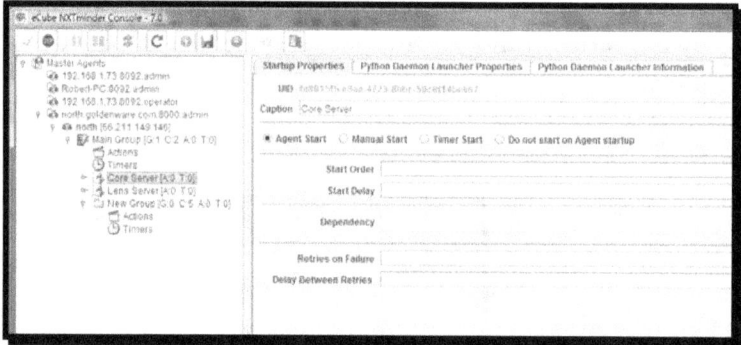

Startup Options:

- **Agent Start:** the Agent will start and stop the Object.
- **Manual Start:** started from the console by clicking the start button.
- **Timer Start:** started by a Start Timer Object.

Start Order: objects are with lower numbers are started first within the Group they belong. You might want to have a higher number than an object that this Object is dependent on.

Start Delay: how long should the object wait to start after the start event is triggered?

Dependency: attach a start and stop dependency based on the status of another object. For example, if the object requires that a Naming Service is up and running, the Object will start and stop based on the status of the Naming Service.

Retries on Failure: number of times the agent will try to start the Object before marking it as having FAILED.

Delay between Retries: time in milliseconds between retries.

Python Daemon Launcher Properties are: (! indicates a mandatory field)

- **! Command:** the command line.
- **Working Directory:** the working directory.
- **Parameters:** command line parameters.
- **! PID File:** the file where the server will store the process identifier.

Health Script properties and usage are described in the Health Script section.

You can add, edit or delete System Environment Variables using the **Add**, **Edit**, or **Delete** buttons.

Action Objects

Actions

Action Objects are used to trigger an event upon a Launcher, a Group or Master Group being started, stopped, or having failed.

Action Objects can be activated or deactivated by checking or un-checking the **Enabled** check box.

File Copy Action

A File Copy Action Object will copy a file from a source directory to a destination directory.

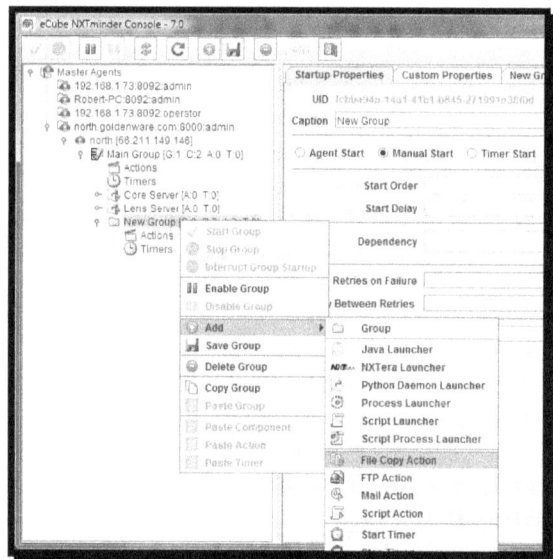

File Copy Action Properties are: (! indicates a mandatory field)

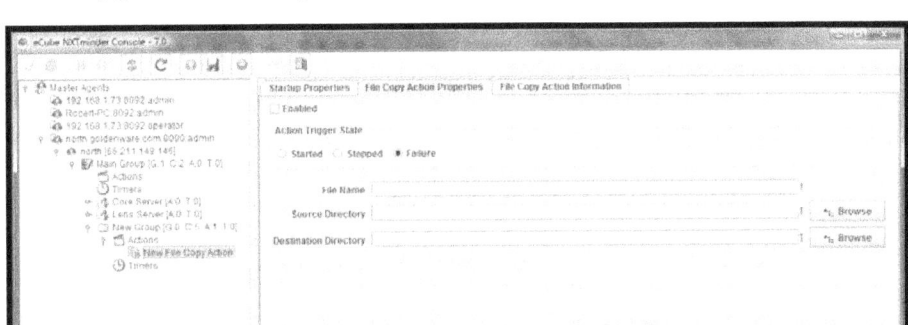

- **! File Name:** the name of the file.
- **! Source Directory:** the source directory.
- **! Destination Directory:** the destination directory

FTP Action

 An FTP Action Object will copy a file to a FTP server.

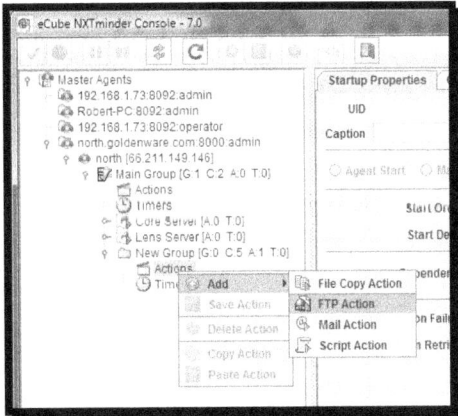

FTP Action Properties are: (! indicates a mandatory field)

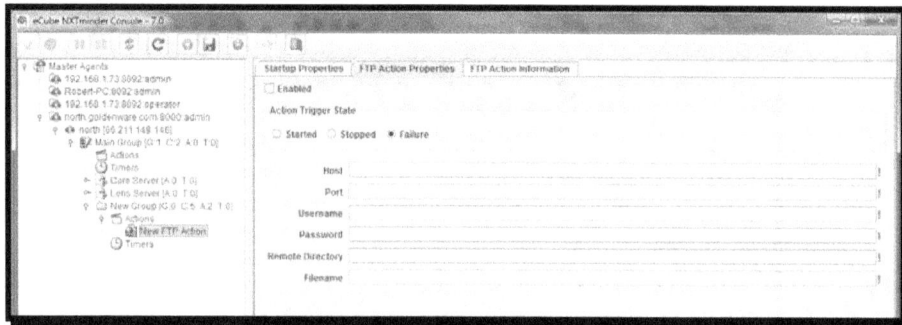

- • **! Host:** the ftp server name or ip address.
- • **! Port:** the ftp server port number.
- • **! Username:** the ftp username.
- • **! Password:** the ftp password.
- • **! Remote Directory:** the destination directory on the ftp server.
- • **! Filename:** the full path and name of the source file to be copied.

Mail Action

A Mail Action Object sends a simple email message. In order to have the Mail Action Object function properly, the mail.host and mail.port proper-ties found in **<Install_Dir>/NXTmonitor_Server or Agent/ properties/mailService.properties** must be set.

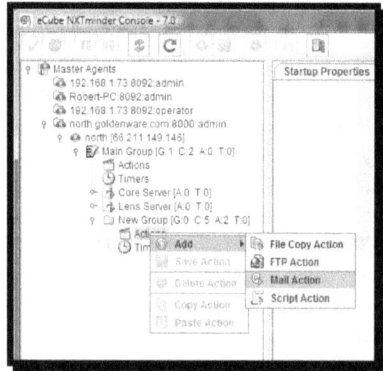

Mail Action Properties are: (! indicates a mandatory field)

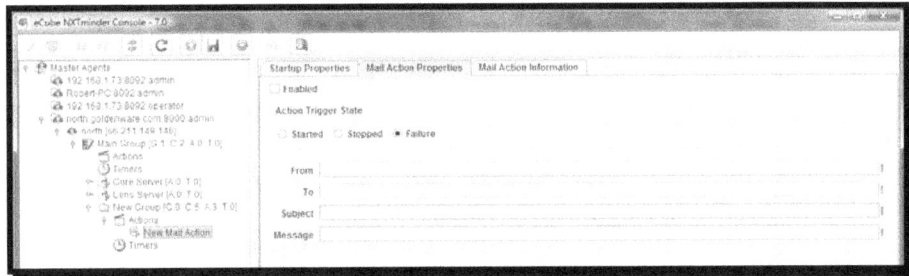

- • **! From:** a valid email address.
- • **! To:** a valid destination email address.
- • **! Subject:** the email subject.
- • **! Message:** the email message.

Script Action

 You use a Script Launcher to execute a script, a bat file, or a process that will not be monitored by NXTmonitor.

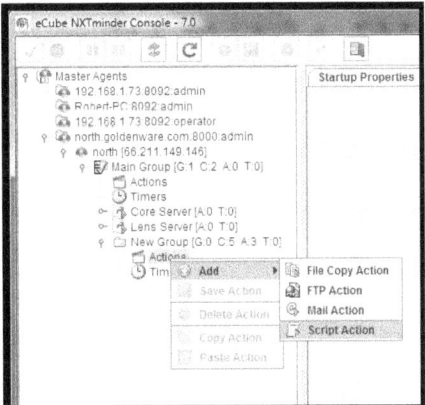

Script Action Properties are: (! indicates a mandatory field)

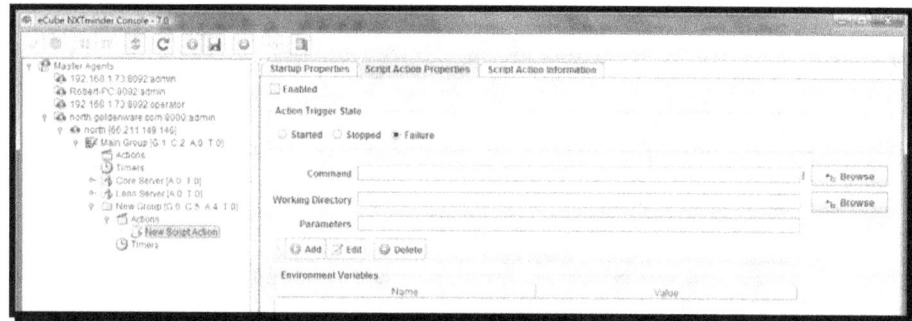

- • **! Command:** the command line.
- • **Working Directory:** the working directory.
- • **Parameters:** command line parameters.

You can add, edit or delete System Environment Variables using the **Add**, **Edit**, or **Delete** buttons.

Timers

Timers are used to manage the start and stopping of managed objects in NXTmonitor. Every Group and Server has a Timer and Actions associated with it and can be customized by the Administrator by entering the information in the Startup Properties tab in the Content window. Timers can be two different types: a starting timer or a stopping timer.

Start Timer

 A Start Timer Object is used to launch a Group or an Object at a certain date and time.

Creating a Start Timer

A time to automatically start and stop applications is created in the NXTmonitor management database. To activate a timer, do the following:

1. Left click on the timer icon to open the two timer settings.

2. for a start timer, click on the Start Timer as shown above.

3. Enter the start and stop times in the navigation panel.

4. Click on the appropriate features for the timer: the list below summarizes your options.

Start Timer Properties are: (! indicates a mandatory field)

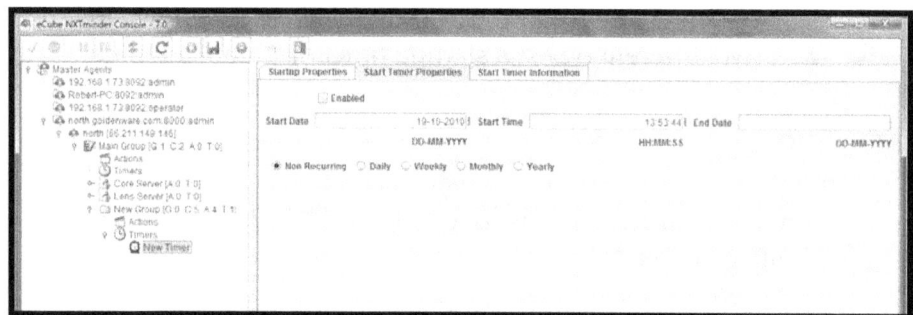

- **! Start Date:** the date the Timer will start.
- **! Start Time:** the time of the day the Timer will start.
- **End Date:** the date the Timer will stop being active.

You must also select the frequency of the Timer.

Non Recurring: gets started once on the Start Date at the Start Time.

Daily:

The screen below is an example of the Timer Properties on Start Timers:

- You can specify the number of days between restart

- You can select to have the Timer start every weekday (Monday through Friday).

- You can select to have the Timer start every weekend. The timer will start only once during the weekend on Saturday or Sunday.

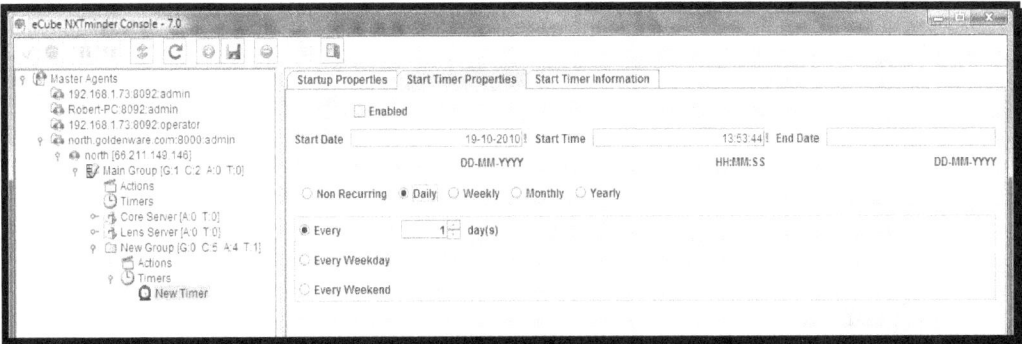

Weekly:

- You can specify the number of weeks between restart.

- You can select one or multiple days of the week for restart.

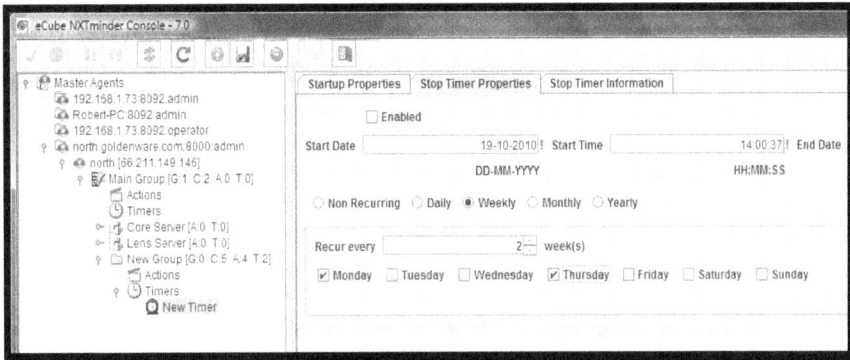

Monthly:

- You can specify the day of the month and the number of months between restart.

- You can specify which specific day of the month and the number of months between restart.

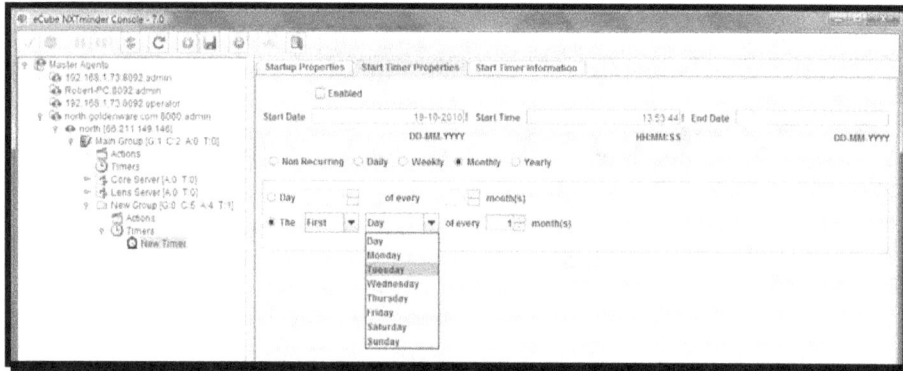

Yearly:

- You can specify the day of the month and the month between restart.

- You can specify which specific day of the month and the month between restart.

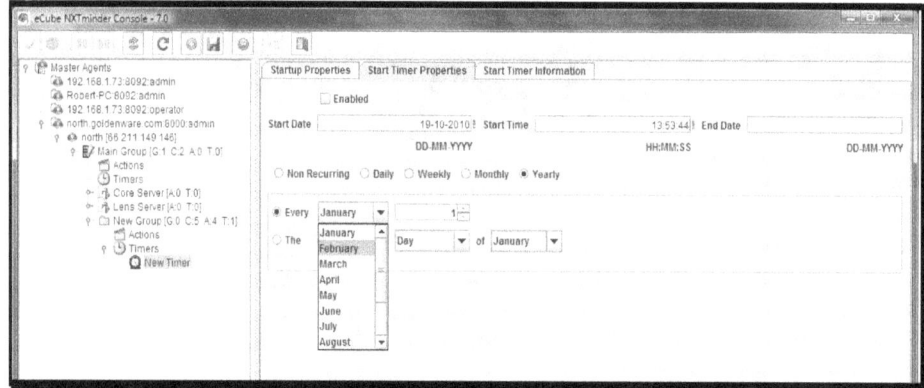

Stop Timer

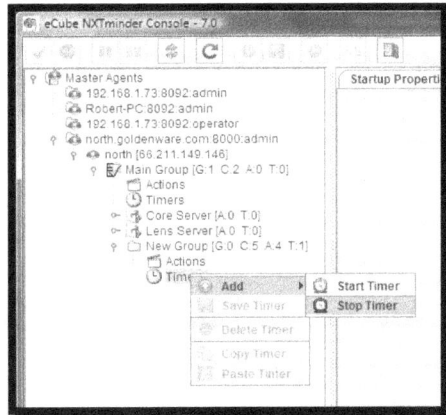

The Stop Timer is a feature that turns off the actions started by a Start Timer. A Stop Timer Object is used to stop a Group or an Object at a certain date and time.

Creating a Stop Timer

A timer to automatically stop actions for applications is created in the NXTmonitor management database. To activate a stop timer, do the follow-ing:

1. Left click on the timer icon to open the two timer settings.

2. For a start timer, click on the Stop Timer as shown above.

3. Enter the start date and times in the navigation panel as shown above.

4. Click on the appropriate features for the timer: the list below summarizes your options.

Stop Timer Properties are: (! indicates a mandatory field)

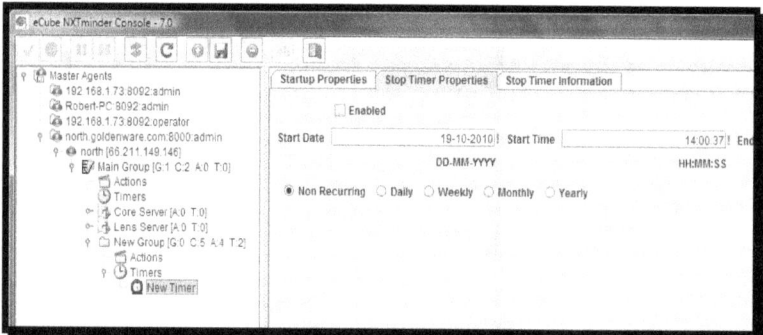

- **! Start Date:** the date the Timer will start the stoppage.
- **! Start Time:** the time of the day the Timer will start the stoppage.
- **End Date:** the date the Timer will stop being active.

You must also select the frequency of the Timer.

Non Recurring: gets started once on the **Start Date** at the **Start Time**.

Daily:

- You can specify the number of days between stoppage
- You can select to have the Timer start the stoppage every weekday (Monday through Friday).

You can select to have the Timer start the stoppage every weekend. The timer will start the stoppage only once during the weekend on Saturday or Sunday.

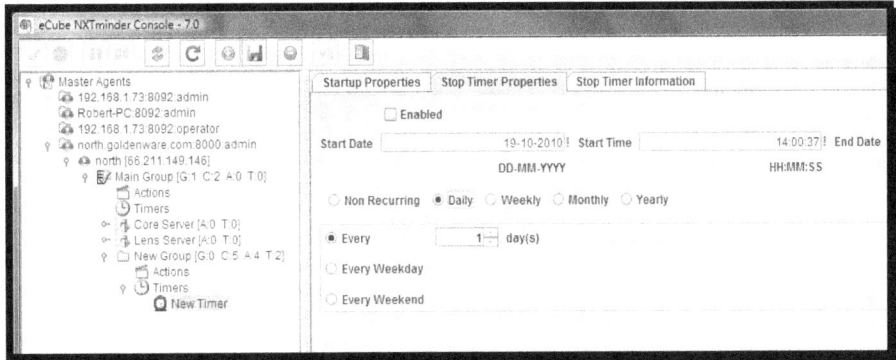

Weekly:

- You can specify the number of weeks between stoppages.
- You can select one or multiple days of the week for stoppage.

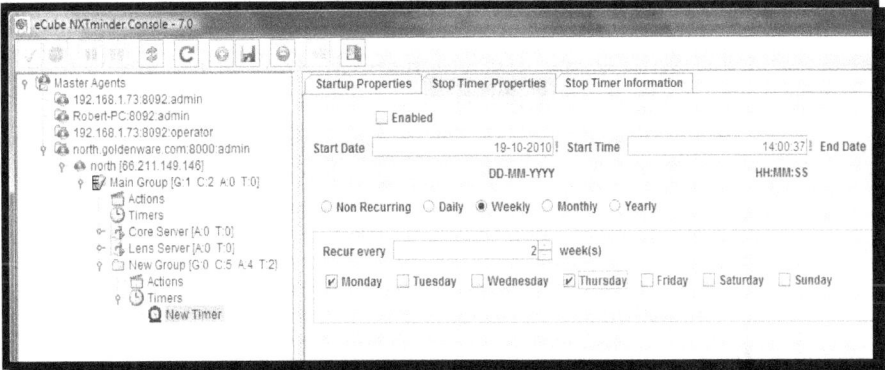

Monthly:

- You can specify the day of the month and the number of months between stoppages.

- You can specify which specific day of the month and the number of months between stoppages.

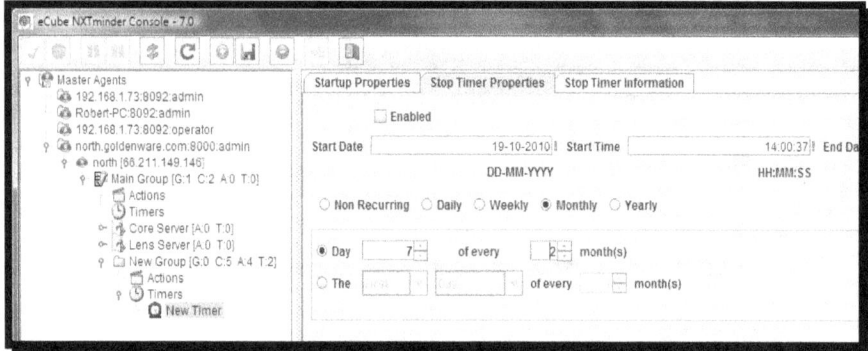

Yearly:

- You can specify the day of the month and the month between stoppages.

- You can specify which specific day of the month and the month between stoppages.

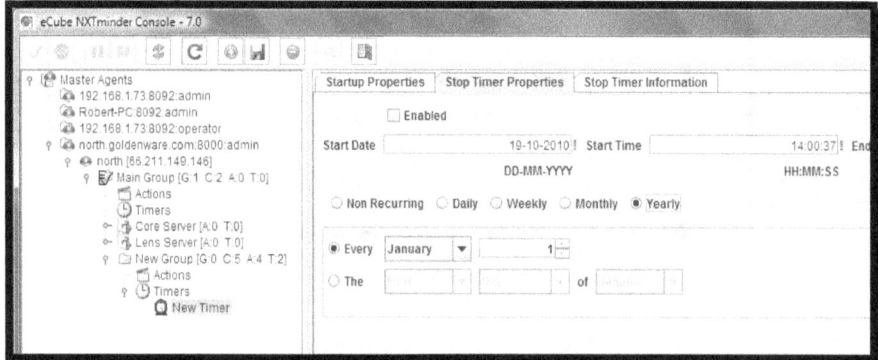

Chapter 5
Using NXTmonitor

This chapter covers how to use NXTmonitor GUI or Console to modify the configuration, change properties for starting and stopping and use of utilities to make sure it is up and running.

Don't forget to start a NXTmonitor agent on every host where NXTmonitor will be monitoring services! (except the host where the Master Server is running) Nothing will work if an agent is not running.

- "Adding a Broker" on page 99.

- "Adding a Server" on page 106.

- "Adding a Database Server" on page 112.

- "Importing Configurations" on page 117.

- "Health Script" on page 119.

- "Supplemental Actions" on page 124.

Logging into the Console

To start using NXTmonitor, you need to log into the Console is the central Graphical User Interface (GUI) for managing NXTmonitor controlled services and objects in an enterprise environment. The Console is also a Java application using Swing components and is the primary source of information for management. The Console GUI is laid out for maximum information display to the analyst and provides instant recognition when problems occur. The layout is a classic three pane layout with menu items and action buttons on the top header of the GUI.

Adding a Broker

What is a Broker?

In the Entera or NXTera middleware world, the Broker is a naming service with which the servers register their bindings. The Broker is like a telephone operator in the Entera or NXTera environment; it keeps a record of servers, so that it can tell clients where to find the servers. No servers or clients can run without it.

When using NXTmonitor under Entera TPC or NXTera, the first item on your agenda must be to add a Broker. The first Broker added to NXTmonitor becomes the Mast Broker by default. The name Master Broker appears at the top of the service list after you add your first Broker.

Before Adding a Broker

If you have not yet started NXTmonitor agent on hosts where NXTmonitor will be monitoring services, do so now!

It's a good idea to make sure that the port which your Broker will use is not already in use by another Broker, or by any other process. Use the netstat command: for instance, if you want to start a Broker at 8888, type:

```
netstat -a |grep 8888
```

to see if port 8888 is occupied.

Add a Master Broker

To add a Broker to your NXTmonitor hierarchy, right click on your server group, go to "**Add**", and select "**NXTera Launcher**" as shown in the picture below. You will notice the right hand content frame contains three tabs for the NXTera Launcher. You need to enter values for each field in the tabs for the NXTera Launcher.

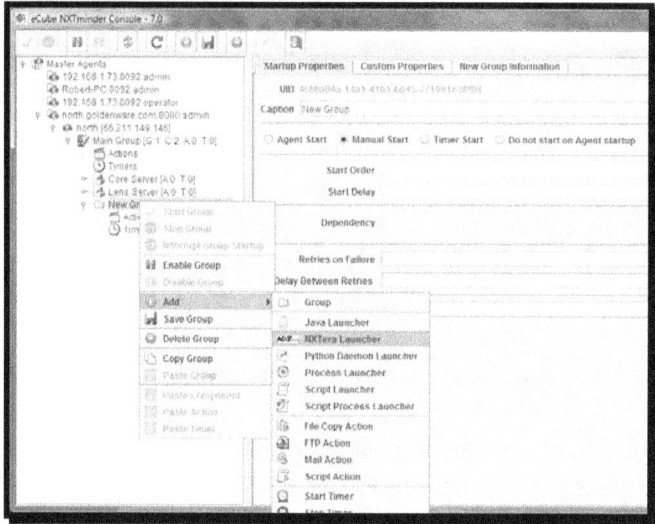

Broker Startup Properties

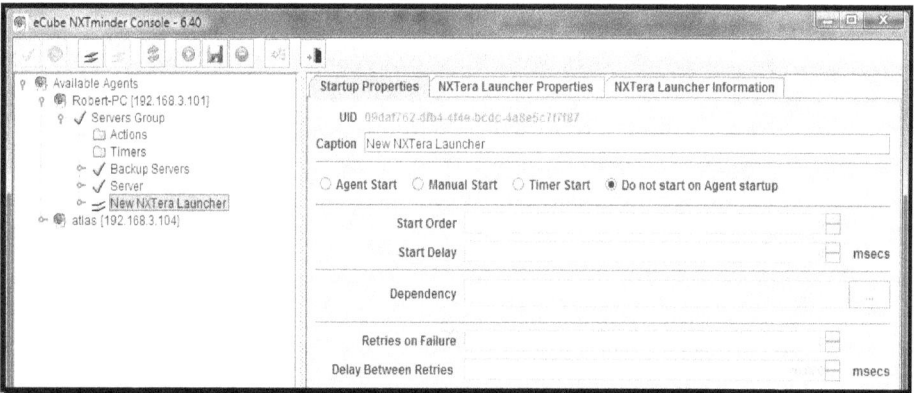

Notice the seven fields for "Caption", Startup Options, "Start Order","Start Delay", "Dependency", "Retries on Failure" and "Delay Between Retries".

The Startup Properties Panel: The startup properties define how the broker will be started. The first field is the Caption, which is where you enter the name to be displayed in the navigation panel. The other fields include start order, start delay, the default status, dependencies, retries and retry delays. A series of radio buttons are used to set the way this broker will be started:

Startup Options are:

- **Agent Start:** the Agent will start and stop the Object.
- **Manual Start:** started from the console by clicking the start button.
- **Timer Start:** started by a Start Timer Object.

Start Order: objects with lower numbers are started first within the Group they belong. You might want to have a higher number than an object that this Object is dependent on.

Start Delay: This time (in milliseconds) is how long should the object wait to start after the start event is triggered.

Dependency: attach a start and stop dependency based on the status of another object. For example, if the object requires that a Naming Service is up and running, the Object will start and stop based on the status of the Naming Service.

Retries on Failure: number of times the agent will try to start the Object before marking it as having FAILED.

Delay between Retries: time in milliseconds between retries

Broker start Launcher Properties

The "Command" needs to be set to "rpcbroker". If you edit this field, the "Broker Start Command" must be set to the basename of the command as you would type it as the command line.

Broker start directory field

The "Working Directory" is preset to the default value of the current directory. This directory is where all of the files needed by the Broker are and identify where the Broker's generated files will go, including the log file and error file. The full path name may not exceed 255 characters.

On OS/2 and Windows NT, the "Working Directory" must be a full path, including drive and directory name. For instance:

```
D:\EXAMPLE\BROKER\FILES
```

Environment files

There are two options for environment files when adding services to NXT-monitor: You may tell NXTmonitor to use an existing file, or you may create a new environment file in the NXTera Workbench Eclipse IDE.

Creating your own environment file

If you don't have an environment file, you will need to create one for the broker to start. The environment file specifies where the Broker is, where the log file will be created and the level of detail to be put into the log.

Here is an example of an environment file:

```
NXT_BROKER=193.1.1.60,7800
NXT_DEBUGLEVEL=DEBUG,DEBUG
NXT_LOG=broker.log
```

If the environment file is not created before the Broker entry is started, NXTmonitor will not be able to start the Broker.

Specifying the environment file

When configuring a NXTera or Entera broker or server, you need to specify the environment file separately rather than an argument on the command line. NXTmonitor constructs the command line from the individual arguments and parameters.

It is essential for NXTmonitor to have accurate knowledge of the information used to start each service. For instance, NXTmonitor treats special servers (dedicated or variable-named) differently then normal servers.

On OS/2 and NT, be sure to provide the full file specification (drive, path and file name) for the environment file. For full details about setting the various environment file values, see the section titled "Environment Files" in Reference.

After you have place valid entries for all the fields in the "NXTera Launcher" content frames and clicked the "SAVE" icon, NXTmonitor will update the configuration frame with the changes you made to ensure it was added successfully.

If there are any immediately detectable errors in the values you have entered in the "Add NXTera Launcher" dialog box, NXTmonitor does not execute the command, and reports the error to you. Some possible errors are:

- The directory specified under "Working Directory" does not exist.
- The host name is invalid.
- The port number is invalid.
- The environment file does not exist (if you are trying to use an existing environment file) or the path to it is incorrect.

If there are no immediate errors, NXTmonitor starts the Broker.

Starting a secure Broker

If NXTmonitor is secure, your Broker must also be secure. For a secure Broker, you must:

- Set   NXT_SECURE=1   in the environment file.

- Fill in the "Broker Key" and "Broker Key Again" fields near the bottom of the "Add Broker" window.

If you are using security, you cannot have sub-Brokers.

Verify the start of the Broker

After you have successfully added a Broker, click the "Start" button to make see if NXTmonitor can launch the new Master Broker.

If NXTmonitor can verify that the Broker is running, it shows the port number of the process in its service list. During the time between NXTmonitor's starting of the Broker and its verification, the service list shows *hosthname*:0 under the "Host:Port" column. After verification, NXTmonitor displays *hostname:portnumber*.

Another way to verify the start of the Broker is to read the `.log` and `.err` files generated by both the Broker and NXTmonitor. The `.log` files contain the RPC log messages generated by the Broker, and the `.err` files contain the Broker's `STDOUT` and `STDERR`.

What happened?

After you completed the "Add Broker" dialog box and clicked OK, NXT-monitor wrote the files it needed (`.run` file, and `.env` file if requested), and executed the `.run` file to start the Broker.

Assuming the Broker came up, it then registered with its parent Broker (unless it was a Master Broker), and wrote output to its `.log` file. The `.err` file was generated automatically, because the Broker's output was directed into the file.

Since the master Broker has successfully started, NXTmonitor can start new services. It also opens its own `.log` file, `netm.log`.

Add another Broker

Click the "Add NXTera Launcher" menu item again to add another Broker. Notice that the "Master Broker Host" and "Master Broker Port" values are already filled in. You can edit these fields to reflect the host and port of any Broker that NXTmonitor has started so far, including the Master Broker.

By adding sub-Brokers, you can easily build a hierarchy for your application. If your application uses OEC security, then you cannot have sub-Broker.

Adding a Server

Before Adding a Server

If you are using NXTera/TCP, remember that NXTmonitor cannot start servers until a Broker is running. After you have successfully added a Mas-ter Broker, try adding a server.

Grayed-out buttons: Keep in mind that, at any given time, only the buttons and fields relevant to the current action or highlighted service are available. For instance, if a server is highlighted in NXTmonitor's list, the "Add NXTera Launcher" (with NXTera/Entera) and the "Add NXTera Launcher " buttons should be grayed out. You cannot add a server to another server, whereas you could add a server to a Broker.

Add NXTera Launcher for a Server

From the main NXTmonitor window, click the "Add NXTera Launcher " button and fill in values for all fields in the "Add NXTera Launcher " content frames.

When the "Add NXTera Launcher " dialog box appears, some of the fields have values in them already. These are defaults set by NXTmonitor. If the text is clear, you may edit the value; if the text is grayed out, the value is fixed.

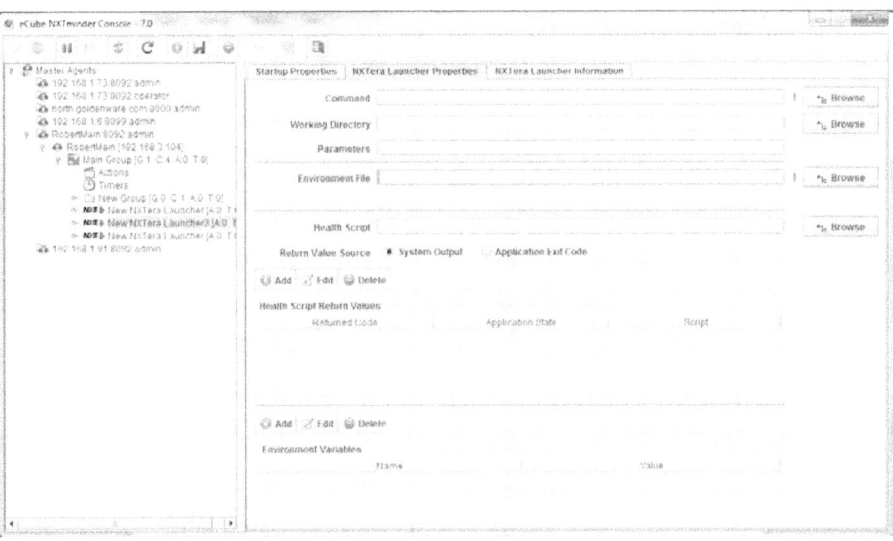

Table 6.1: Properties of NXTera startup Launcher Tab Fields

Field Name	Properties
Caption	Name of NXTera Launcher
Startup Options	• Agent Start: the Agent will start and stop the Object.
	• Manual Start: started from the console by clicking the start button.
	• Timer Start: started by a Start Timer Object.
Start Order	Objects with lower numbers are started first within the Group they belong. You might want to have a higher number than an object that this Object is dependent on.
Start Delay	How long should the object wait to start after the start event is triggered?

Table 6.1: Properties of NXTera startup Launcher Tab Fields

Field Name	Properties
Dependency	Attach a start and stop dependency based on the status of another object. For example, if the object requires that a Naming Service is up and running, the Object will start and stop based on the status of the Naming Service.
Retries on Failure	This is the number of times the agent will try to start the Object before making it as having FAILED.
Delay between Retries	The time in milliseconds between retries.
Start Command	(Mandatory) The command line to execute the application goes here.
Working Directory	(Mandatory) The working directory where the application will store its files is entered here.
Parameters	Extra command line parameters besides the -e <envFile>.
Environment File	(Mandatory) The Entera or NXTera environment file.
Environment Variables	Use the buttons provided in this section to Add, Edit, or Delete Environment Variables

The values for "Initial Delay", "Ping Period", and "Max # Retries" can also be changed later, through the "Service Info" button. See "Service Information" for more information.

NXTera/TCP specific options

Table 6.2: NXTera/TCP specific server startup options

Field Name	What Contents Should Be
Broker Host Name	Values are preset to the values of the Master Broker. You may change the values to those of any Broker that was started through NXTmonitor.

Table 6.2: NXTera/TCP specific server startup options

Field Name	What Contents Should Be
Broker Host Port	Values are preset to the values of the Master Broker. You may change the values to those of any Broker that was started through NXTmonitor.
Ping Function Name	Name of the RPC that NXTmonitor uses to ping the server. The field value is set to nxt_ping() by default, since all ser-vices should be able to respond to it. You can change the calue to any other function name, as long as it is one that the server can recognize and respond to. The only stipulation is that the function must follow this format: int function(void). In other words, the function must take no arguments, and must return an integer value.
Ping Return Value	The value that is returned by the "Ping Function". In the case of nxt_ping(1), the value is one (1).
Broker Key / Broker Key Again	If you are using security, these text fields must be filled in correctly. Passwords must not begin with a space, and must be longer than 8 characters on UNIX and NT, or longer than 5 characters on OS/2.
User Password / Password Again	If you are using security, these text fields must be filled in correctly. Passwords must not begin with a space, and must be longer than 8 characters on UNIX and NT, or longer than 5 characters on OS/2.

Environment Files

There are two options for environment files when adding services to NXT-monitor: You may tell NXTmonitor to use an existing file, or you may create a new environment file in the NXTera Workbench Eclipse IDE.

Creating your own environment file

If you don't have an environment file, you will need to create one for the broker to start. The environment file specifies where the Broker is, where the log file will be created and the level of detail to be put into the log.

Here is an example of an environment file:

```
NXT_BROKER=193.1.1.60,7800
NXT_DEBUGLEVEL=DEBUG,DEBUG
NXT_LOG=broker.log
```

If the environment file is not created before the Server entry is started, NXTmonitor will not be able to start the Server.

Specifying the environment file

When configuring a NXTera or Entera broker or server, you need to specify the environment file separately rather than an argument on the command line. NXTmonitor constructs the command line from the individual arguments and parameters.

It is essential for NXTmonitor to have accurate knowledge of the information used to start each service. For instance, NXTmonitor treats special servers (dedicated or variable-named) differently then normal servers.

On OS/2 and NT, be sure to provide the full file specification (drive, path and file name) for the environment file. For full details about setting the various environment file values, see the section titled "Environment Files" in Reference.

After you have place valid entries for all the fields in the "NXTera Launcher" content frames and clicked the "SAVE" icon, NXTmonitor will update the configuration frame with the changes you made to ensure it was added successfully.

If there are any immediately detectable errors in the values you have entered in the "Add NXTera Launcher" dialog box, NXTmonitor does not execute the command, and reports the error to you. Some possible errors are:

- The directory specified under "Working Directory" does not exist.

- The host name is invalid.

- The port number is invalid.

- The environment file does not exist (if you are trying to use an existing environment file) or the path is wrong.

If there are no immediate errors, NXTmonitor attempts to start the server.

Verify the Start of the Server

After you have successfully added a Server, click the "Start" button to make see if NXTmonitor can launch the new Server.

If NXTmonitor can verify that the server is running, it shows the port number of the process in its service list. After starting the server, but before verifying it, the service list shows *hostname*:0 for that server. After verification, NXTmonitor shows *hostname:portnumber* for that server.

What happened?

After you completed the "Add NXTera Launcher" content frame and clicked the "SAVE" icon, NXTmonitor wrote the files it needed (.run file, .env file, if requested), and executed the .run file to start the server.

Assuming the server came up, it then registered with its Broker and wrote output to its .log file. The .err file was generated automatically because the server's output was directed into the file.

Adding a Database Server

Because database servers require special preparation for their environment (namely different settings of environment variables) before they run, we recommend that you write a small script which does the preparation, and then invokes the server. When you have finished the script, be sure to give it executable permissions.

The form of this shell should be the following if you use Bourne Shell (sh) or Korn Shell (ksh):

```
*************begin: start-up script*************
export VARIABLE1=value1
export VARIABLE2=value2
.
.
[commands which set up configuration files, etc.]
.
.
my_server $*
*************end: start-up script*************
```

The syntax should resemble the following for C Shell (csh) or TC Shell (tcsh):

```
*************begin: start-up script*************
sentenv VARIABLE1=value1
sentenv VARIABLE2=value2
.
.
[commands which set up configuration files, etc.]
.
.
my_server $*
*************end: start-up script*************
```

On OS/2 or Windows NT, the equivalent command file (.CMD) syntax would be:

```
*************begin: myserver cmd file*************
SET VARIABLE1=value1
SET VARIABLE2=value2
.
.
.
[commands which set up configuration files, etc.]
.
.
.
my_server -e server.env
*************end: myserver cmd file*************
```

Since OS/2 and Windows NT environment variables only apply to the current command session, you should not use START or DETATCH to start servers in command files.

Example

An Oracle database server requires the following environment variables to be set: ORACLE_HOME, ORACLE_SID, PATH. In order for the database server (ora_start) to be successfully invoked, these variables must be in its environment. When starting ora_start from a command line, you can type something like the following:

```
>ORACLE_HOME=/users/oracle; export ORACLE_HOME
>ORACLE_SID=demo7f; export ORACLE_SID
PATH=$PATH:$ORACLE_HOME/bin; export PATH
ora_start -q orders.qfile -d demo7f -s demo -e orders.env
```

In face, you would probably put those environment variable lines into your .profile or .login so that they would be run for you automatically each time you log in.

However, if you had two different databases on your machine, then you would have to change the value of ORACLE_SID in order to start a server that used a different database. For example, if you had a database called prod7f (which contains the production data) as well as the demo7f (which contains the demo data), then you might now type something like:

```
>ORACLE_SID=prod7f; export ORACLE_SID
>ora_start -q orders.qfile -d prod7f -s prod -e
   orders.env
```

which changes the value of ORACLE_SID in the environment, and then starts another server.

Making the Script

If you had to shift between databases often, it would be convenient to put these commands into a shell script or command line file - an executable file which contains system commands - and then just run the script each time. You can create a file, prodstart, which contains these two lines. Add one more line to the beginning of the file to specify the kind of shell in which the script should execute, and your file should look similar to this one:

```
#!/bin/sh
ORACLE_SID=prod7f; export ORACLE_SID
ora_start -q orders.qfile -d produ7f -s prod -e
    orders.env
```

Now if you type:

```
>prodstart
```

the script exports the Oracle environment variable for you, then invokes ora_start with the correct commands. By typing only one line, you save time and effort. However, you might want to rapidly change back and forth between two different database environments, without having to edit the script. In that case you could modify the ora_start line inside the file to look like this:

```
ora_start -q orders.qfile -d prod7f -s prod -e $1
```

The $1 is replaced with whatever parameter you type on the command line. Thus if you now type:

```
prodstart abc.env
```

abc.env is substituted for $1, so your server uses abc.env as its environment file.

In fact, you may want to control more than that, so you can change the ora-start line inside the file to:

```
ora_start -q orders.qfile -d newdata $*
```

and now all the arguments that you put on the command line for prod-start are used in the ora_start line. Thus if you type:

```
>prodstart -e newbroker.env -s newname
```

then the actual command line executes is:

```
ora_start -q orders.qfile -d newdata -e newbroker.env
     -s newname
```

This is the usual way of "parameterizing" a shell script.

Using the Script with NXTmonitor

Now that you have your script, you need to use it within NXTmonitor. What you need to decide in parameterizing your script is the following:

- what information are you going to want to specify from NXT-monitor

- what information is only interesting to the administrator and not the developer

- what information is only interesting to the developer and not the administrator

The first two types of information should be parameterized, so that the administrator can modify them from within NXTmonitor. The last type of information should be recorded in the script so that they are invisible to the administrator, who doesn't have to worry about them.

In the example above, the name of the "qfile" and the database name are of no concern to the administrator, so they belong in the script. However, the server name is of prime importance to the administrator, who must know about any potential conflicts between servers, so the server name should be parameterized. For flexibility, the environment file name should be param-eterized as well.

From within NXTmonitor you would now specify the start-up command in the "Server Start Command" field as:

```
prodstart -s newname -e order.env
```

or something to the like, so that if you want to change the server's name, or the environment file it is using, you do not need to modify the script, you only need to modify the NXTmonitor configuration.

More detailed information on these three options, See "Verify the start of the Broker" on page 104. Also, you can check to see that the sever process is up and running by using the UNIX ps command.

Importing Configurations

NXTmonitor is a successor product to NetMinder and Appminder. As one of its features, it provides the ability to import an AppMinder configuration. See the highlighted Import icon below:

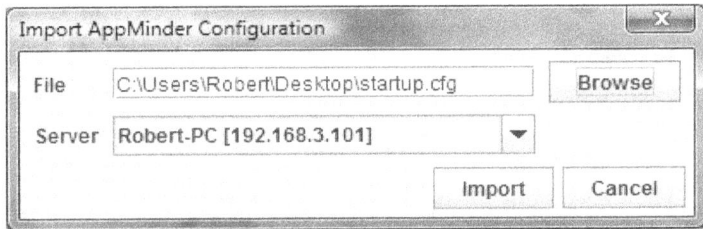

When this screen is shown, select the configuration (.cfg) file that you previously exported from the AppMinder management console.

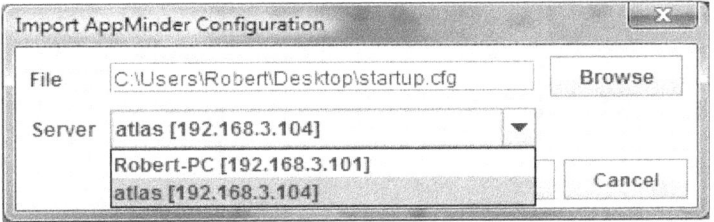

Select the server where you wish to import the configuration.

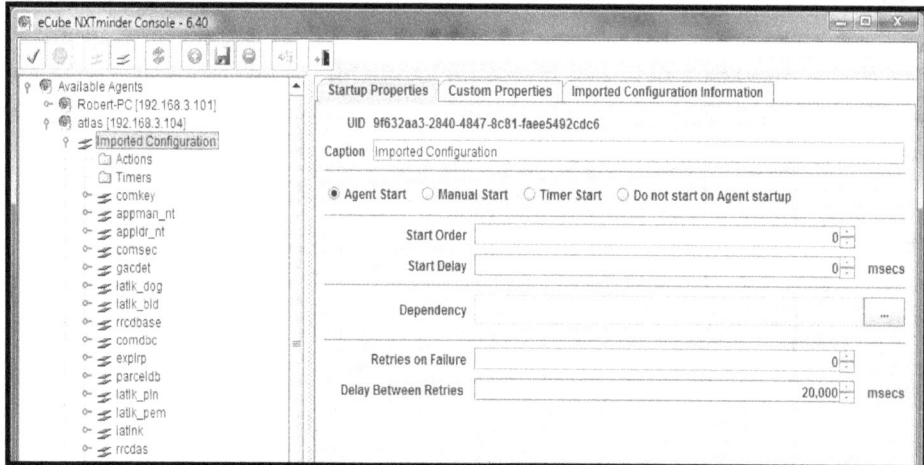

Health Script

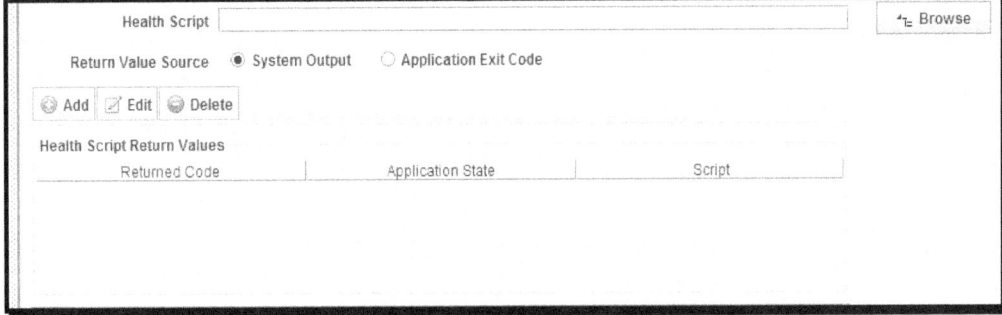

A process may not be responsive even if it's status is up. You can specify a
health script that will be executed every time the object gets pinged. The
health script can be a script or an executable that returns a code. The code
can be returned in one of the following ways:

- **System Output**: The returned code must have the following format
  on a single line.

  ReturnCode=[return code]

- **Application Exit Code**: The **exit status** or **return code** of the process used has the health script.

You can set an object state based on the returned code and trigger a script
or an executable based on a certain state.

Health Script Return Values

Returned code values are added, edited or deleted using the buttons on the
toolbar. When adding a new entry, the following dialog box will appear.

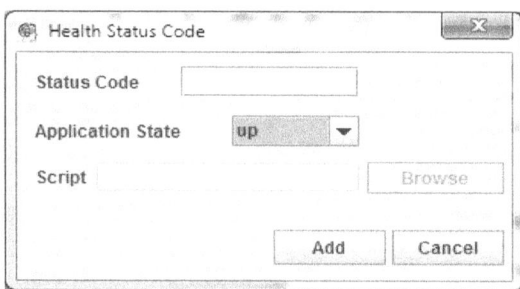

1. Enter a Status Code and select an Application State. The choices are [up, failed, process].

2. If "process" is selected, enter a script or an executable in the Script field.

An Application State of "failed" or "process" will trigger a stoppage of the object by the agent.

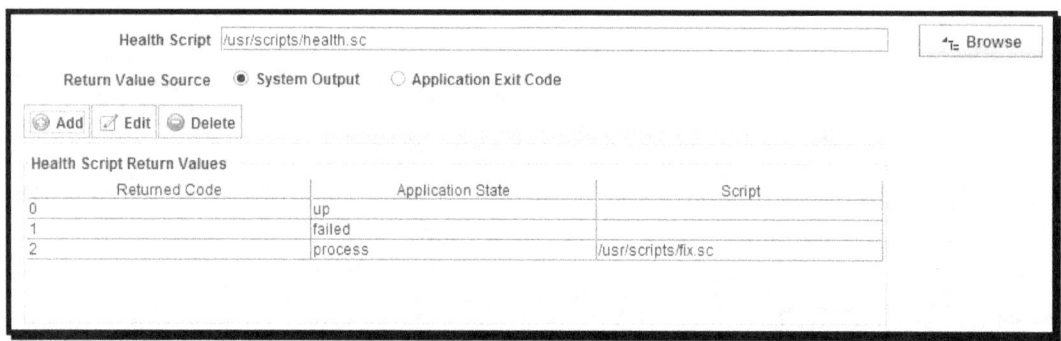

Importing

NXTmonitor provides the ability to import an AppMinder configuration.

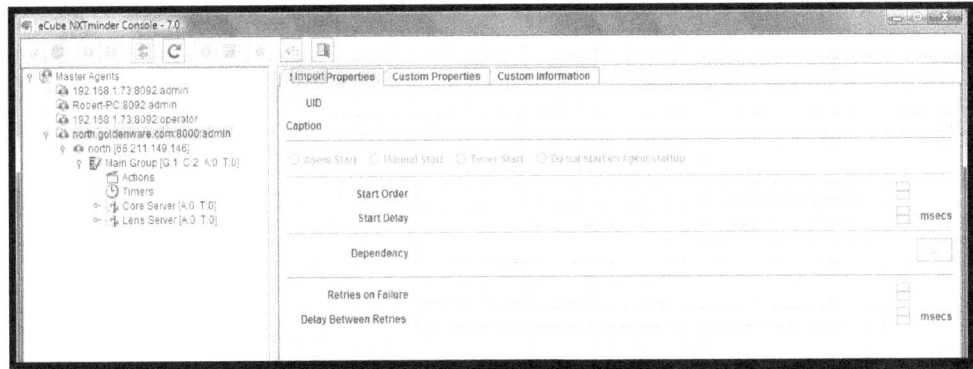

Select the configuration (.cfg) file that you previously exported from AppMinder.

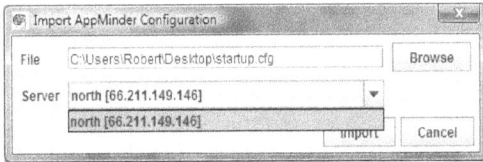

Select the server where you wish to import the configuration.

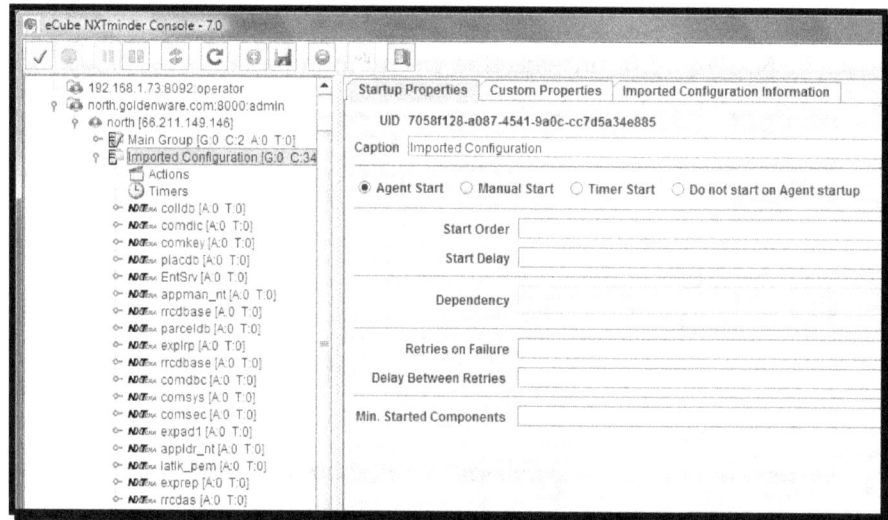

Duplicating Components and Actions

Components, including Groups and Actions can be duplicated. Select the item that you wish to duplicate and right click.

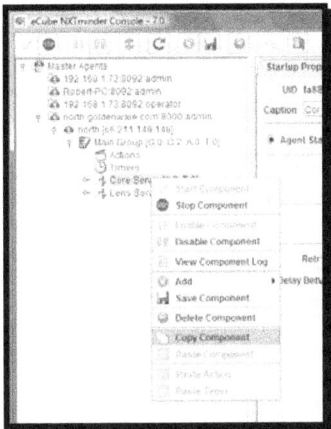

Select the group where you wish to copy the component and right click. Select Paste <Object Type>.

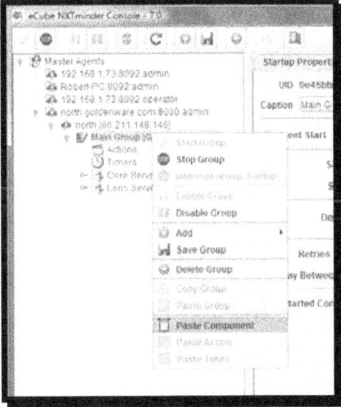

Note: Master Groups cannot be duplicated.

Supplemental Actions

Adding Brokers, adding services, and adding incrementing and decrementing servers are the actions most often used within NXTmonitor. Here are the other functions NXTmonitor can perform.

Testing an Agent

To make sure an agent is responding well to NXTmonitor, click the "Test Agent" button. When prompted with the "Test Agent" dialog box, enter a hostname and click "OK". NXTmonitor attempts to contact the agent on that host. It then reports on the status of the communication between the two processes.

Pinging a Service

In AppCenter or Appminder, to make sure a server or Broker is running, highlight the server instance or Broker on NXTmonitor's list, and then you had to click the "Ping Service" button. While AppCenter is pinging a server, its GUI freezes. When the ping is finished, a dialog box appears, indicating whether or not the service is running. For performance reasons, this functionality is automatically provided by NXTmonitor and is done in the background.

Killing a Service

In order to stop all instances of a particular service, select that service from NXTmonitor's service list and click the "Stop" button. NXTmonitor makes sure this is what you want to do before stopping each instance of the service you selected.

Killing a Broker (NXTera/TCP only)

If you choose a Broker, NXTmonitor stops the Broker as well as all services that have registered with it through NXTmonitor.

To kill a Broker, select it from the service list and press the "Stop" button. NXTmonitor prompts you to make sure you want to stop this process. If you have chosen the Master Broker, NXTmonitor prompts you twice. Removing the Master Broker removes all currently active services in your distributed application that have registered with that Master Broker through NXTmonitor.

When you tell NXTmonitor to kill a Broker, it removes all of the services registered to that Broker before it kills the Broker itself.

To kill the Broker, NXTmonitor first tries to connect to it. If it connects successfully, NXTmonitor issues a `nxt_close()` RPC to bring down the service gracefully. If the connect fails, then NXTmonitor issues a `SIGINT` signal to the Broker's process ID to bring it down.

Killing a Server

When you choose a server and press the "STOP" button, NXTmonitor stops all services with the same interface name. NXTmonitor does not stop services that it is not managing.

In response to the "Stop," NXTmonitor removes each instance, once at a time. To kill and instance, NXTmonitor goes through exactly the same pro-cess as killing a Broker (see page 125): first try to bring down the server with an RPC, if that fails, send a `SIGINT` signal to bring it down.

When all instances of a server have been killed, it is not possible to incre-ment it again until it has been added back through the "Add Server" dialog box.

Service Information

NXTmonitor allows you to get the information about a particular service, such as its location (`hostname:portnumber`), process ID, debug level, which Broker it is registered with, etc. To get this information, select the service from the service list and click the "Service Info" button.

Once a server or Broker has been started, you can make some changes to it. Some of these changes take effect immediately, while others take effect only when the server is restarted.

Within the "Service Info" box, you edit certain characteristics of a service. If the text box is 3D, it can be edited. If you make changes and want to commit them, press the "Change" button. Press the "Don't Change" to cancel any alterations you have made.

Making Changes to a Broker (NXTera/TCP only)

The following fields cannot be changed for a Broker: "Broker Name", "Broker Host Name", "Broker Host Port", "Parent Broker Host", and "Parent Broker Port". All other fields can be changed, but the changes do not take effect until NXTmonitor restarts the Broker.

The "Broker Info" window looks just like the "Add Broker" window, except that some fields are not editable.

Making Changes to a Server

For servers, most fields can be changed. The ones that are unchangeable are the server's host and port number, and the host and port number of the Broker to which the server registers.

If you make changes to the values in the "Initial Delay", "Ping Period" or "Max # Retries" fields, NXTmonitor take the alterations into account immediately. Changes to other fields do not have an effect until NXTmonitor restarts the service.

The "Server Info" window looks exactly like the "Add Server" window.

Why Some Changes only Take Effect when the Service is Restarted

All of a services's information is updated within NXTmonitor's internal table when you click the "Change" button in the "Service Information" window. The changes do not have an effect until NXTmonitor reads its internal table again. It only reads its internal table when it has to restart a service. Some fields, such as the ping related ones, are used so often by NXTmonitor that the changes affect each service almost immediately. Oth-ers, such as the "Server Start Command", are used only at start-up.

For example, changing the start directory of a server from /usr/perales to /usr/perales/test does not make the server that is currently running in /usr/perales change the directory in which it runs. After you have made the change to the service's information, NXTmonitor starts the server from the new directory the next time it attempts a restart.

The most frequent use of the capability to change a service's information is when you have made a mistake in the "Add Server" or "Add Broker" window. Imagine you want to start a server from /usr/perales/test, but type only /usr/perales in the "Server Start Directory" field of the "Add Server" window. NXTmonitor tries to start the server and fails. Check the service information, discover your typing mistake, and fix it. During the next ping cycle, NXTmonitor attempts a restart from the new (correct) directory.

Reader Buttons

Included with NXTmonitor is a file reading program, called reader. This utility works on OS/2 and UNIX platforms; the Windows NT version of NXTmonitor uses NotePad. With reader, you can look at the error and log files generated for NXTmonitor and all the services it monitors. All you have to do is select a service and click a button.

There are four buttons on the NXTmonitor GUI that access reader. They are labeled "Netm Log File", Netm Error File", "Service Log File", and "Service Error File". The titles of the buttons explain the functions they perform. To use the "Service Log File" and "Service Error File" buttons, select a service from the service list, then click the one of the buttons. For more information on the reader utility, see **"Using the reader GUI"**

Informational Buttons

The topmost row of buttons on the GUI are informational in nature. If you click one, it tells you what information is written in the column underneath it.

Another information-providing button is the one labeled "NXTmonitor Info". When you click it, an interactive message box appears with NXTmonitor's hostname, port number, and process ID (PID), the port number at which NXTmonitor expects to find its agents, and NXTmonitor's current configuration file; it also tells you if the NXTmonitor RPC API is activated, and if NXTmonitor is locked; the third type of information is the current debugging levels for NXTmonitor. If a particular bit of information is not grayed-out, you may change it in this window.

The last button on the GUI is labeled "Clear Messages". It clears the message line at the bottom of the GUI.

Chapter 6
NXTmonitor Mobile

A mobile phone interface enabling you to start and stop configurations, groups or processes is available. The connection is done through the NXTmonitor client servlet and the NXTmonitor Web Service. The following section presents three possible deployment solutions. The port numbers are the default being used by the different components. They can be changed to satisfy your specific requirements.

- "Deployment Architecture" on page 131.

- "Deploying the mobile components" on page 134.

- "Web Client Packages" on page 134.

- "Generating and deploying the Web Service" on page 135.

- "Using the mobile application" on page 137.

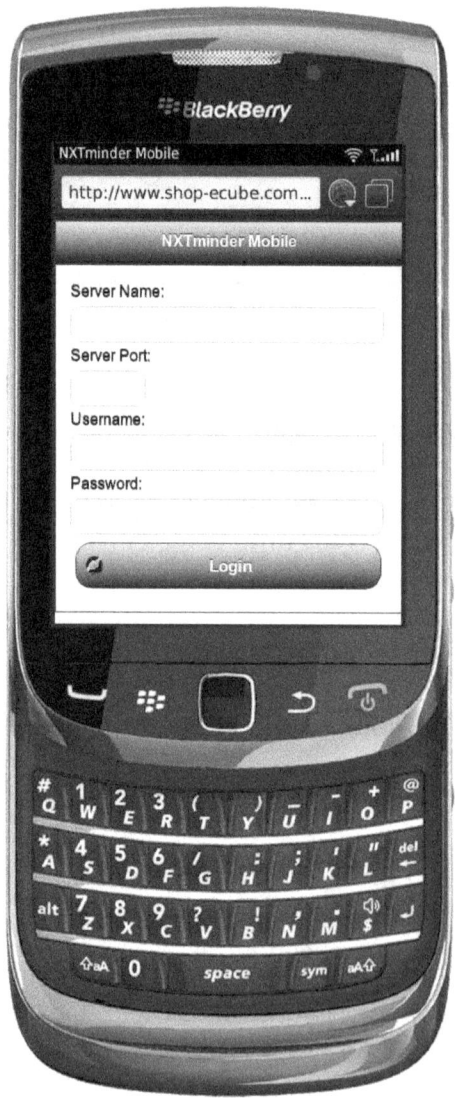

Deployment Architecture

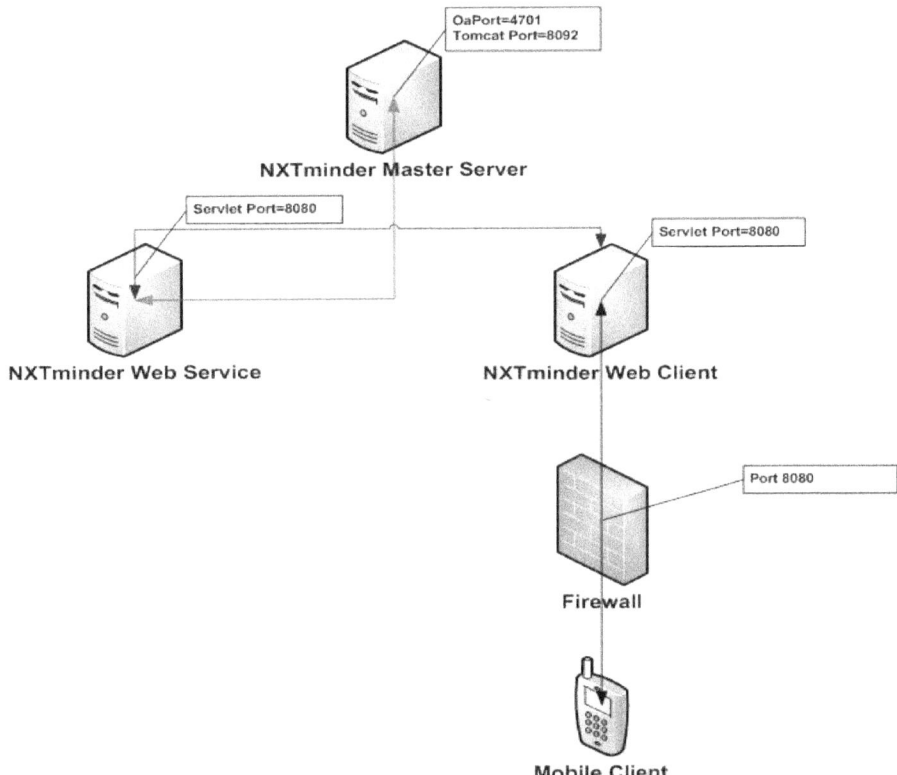

This option has all of the components running inside the firewall. The firewall must allow the traffic to access the NXTmonitor Web Client listening port or rout the request.

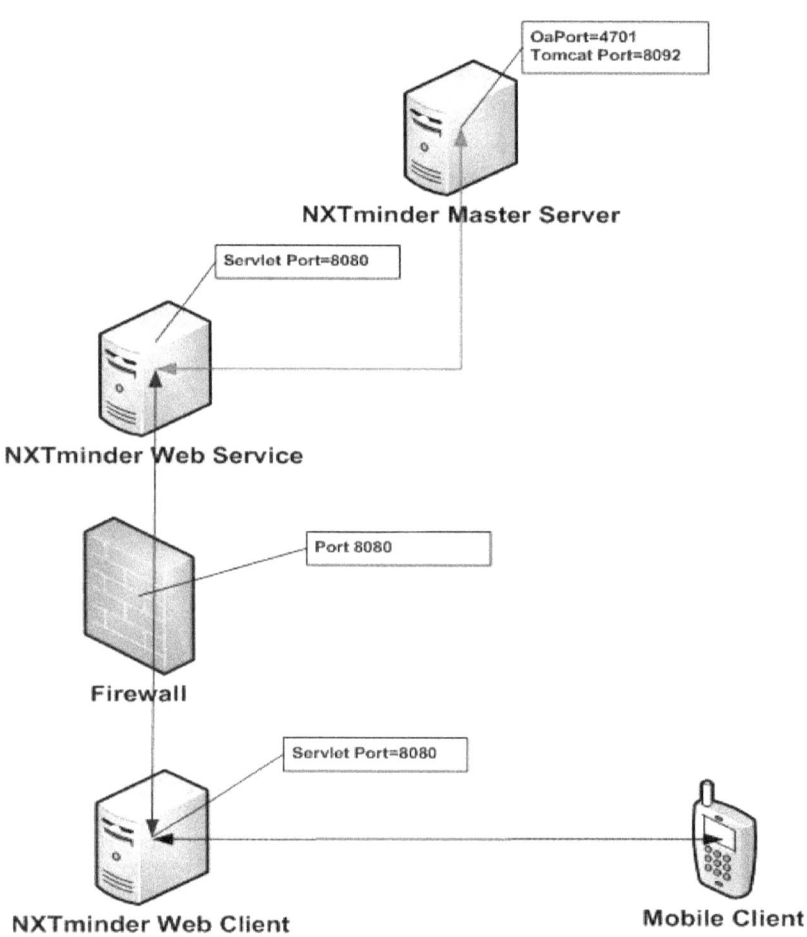

NXTminder Master Server

NXTminder Web Service

Firewall

NXTminder Web Client   Mobile Client

This option has the NXTmonitor Web Client outside the firewall. The firewall must allow the traffic to access the NXTmonitor Web Service listening port or rout the request.

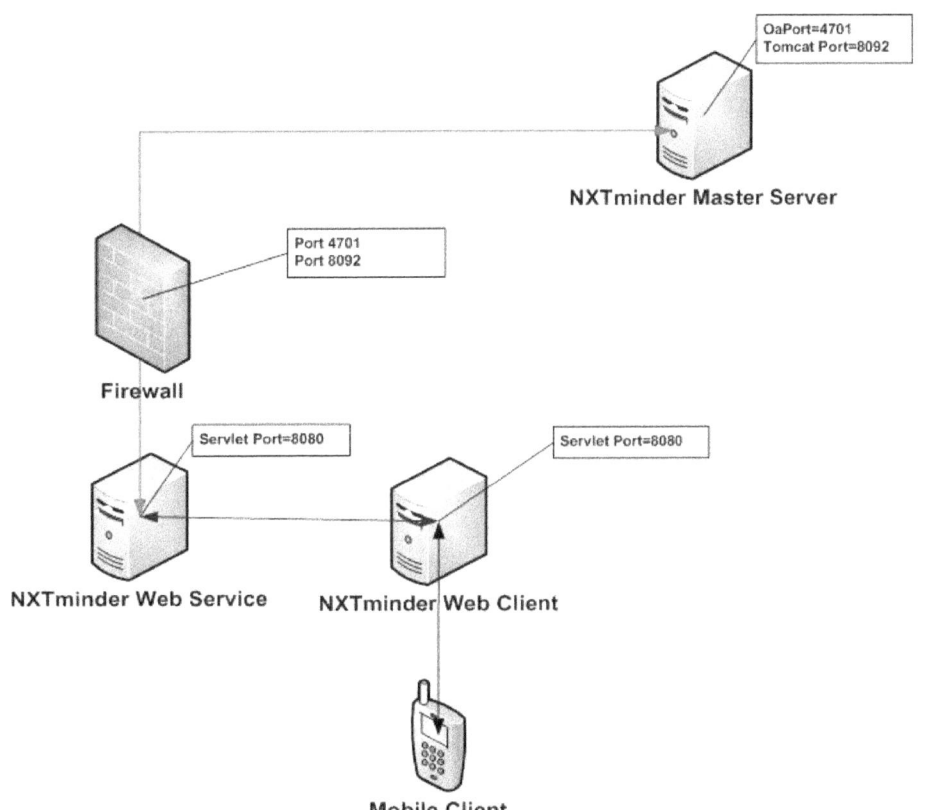

This option has the NXTmonitor Web Service and the NXTmonitor Web Client outside the firewall. The firewall must allow the traffic to access the NXTmonitor Master Server listening ports or rout the request. This option requires two ports to be open.

Deploying the mobile components

The NXTmonitor Web Service packages and the NXTmonitor Web Client are both java based and they require a J2EE servlet engine in order to run.

Web Service Packages

The NXTmonitor installation zip file contains a directory named mobile. Unzip the content of the **mobile.zip** file in the servlet webapps directory.

⊿ webapps
 ▷ docs
 ▷ examples
 ▷ host-manager
 ▷ manager
 ▷ mobile

Web Client Packages

The NXTmonitor installation zip file contains a directory named mobile. Unzip the content of the **nxtminderMobile.zip** file in the servlet webapps directory.

⊿ webapps
 ▷ docs
 ▷ examples
 ▷ host-manager
 ▷ manager
 ▷ mobile
 ▷ nxtminderMobile

Generating and deploying the Web Service

Generating

The Web Service component is generated using the **NXTmonitor console**.

Start by selecting a **Master Agent**.

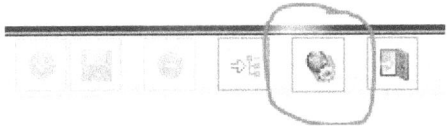

Click on the **Generate Web Service** button found on the toolbar.

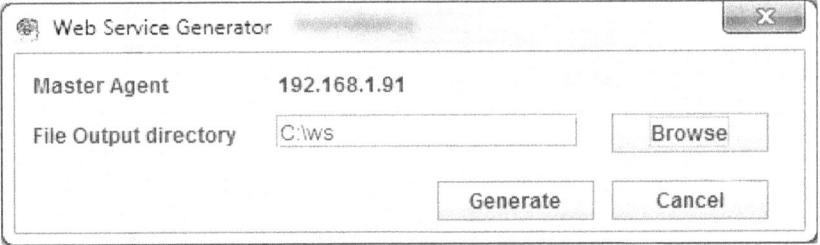

Enter the output location of the generated web archive and click **Generate**.

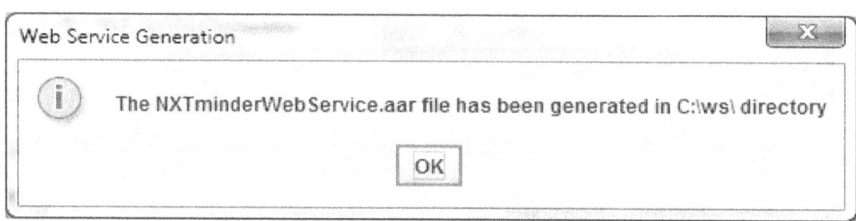

Deploying

Copy the NXTmonitorWebService.aar file generated previously into the **<servlet>/webapps/mobile/WEB-INF/services** directory.

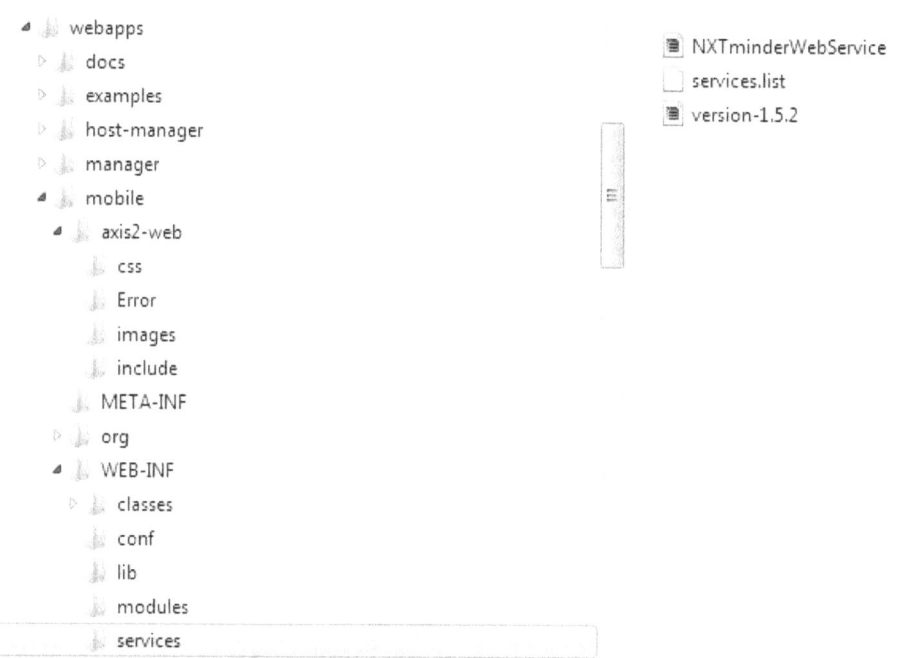

Using the mobile application

You access the NXTmonitor Mobile Application by using your mobile phone web browser. Enter the following URL:

http://<web client address>:<web client port>/nxtmonitorMobile/cli-ent/

Refer to the **Deployment Architecture** section for the details about the web client address and port.

The following screen should appear:

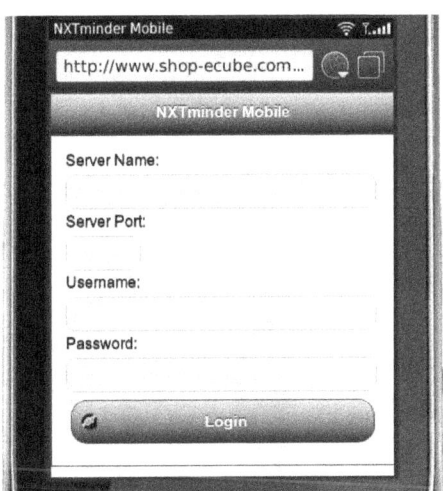 

- The **Server Name** is the URL of the Web Service.
- The **Server Port** is the http listening port of the servlet.
- The **Username** cannot be admin. Refer to the NXTmonitor **Administration** section for more details.

Upon a successful login, the different agents associated with the Web Service will be listed. Below is the same listing displayed with the **console**.

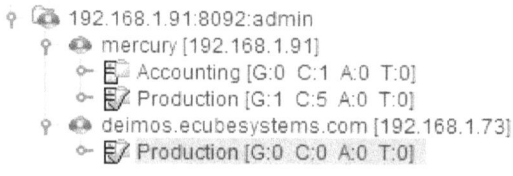

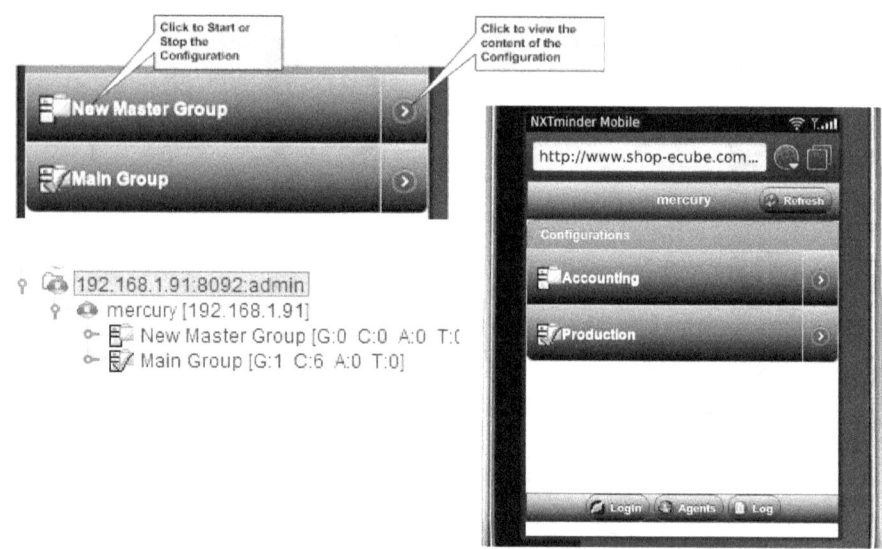

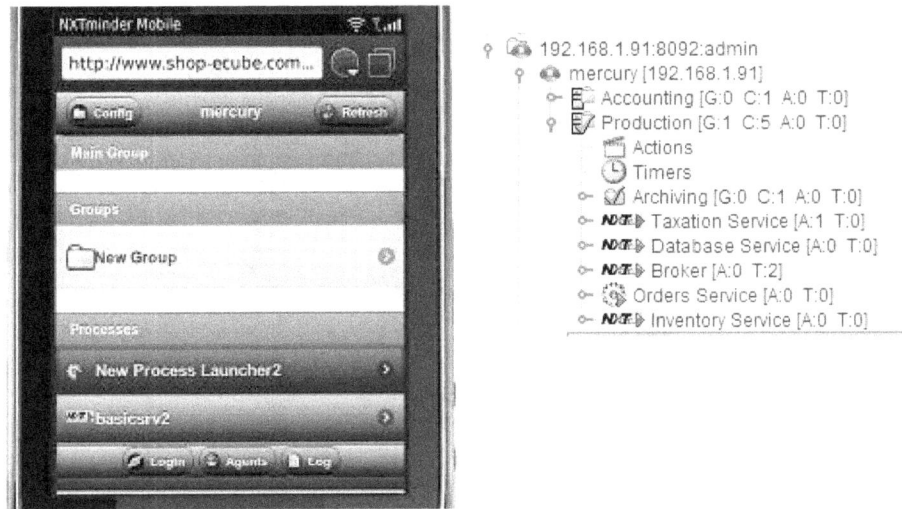

The content of a Group is divided into two sections, the **Groups** and the **Processes**.

The status icons are identical to the icons used in the console.

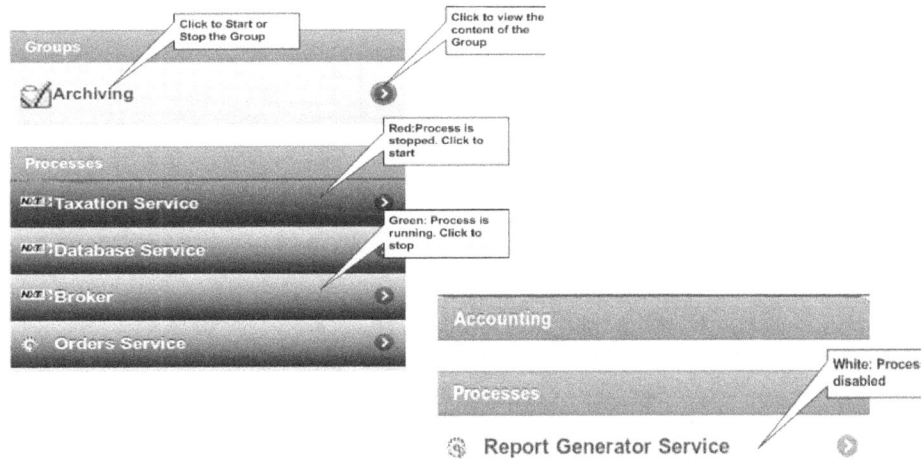

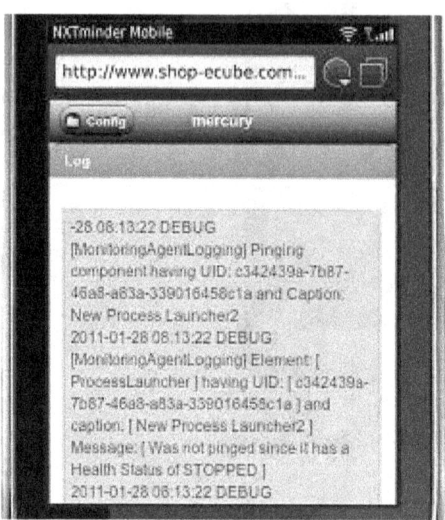

The log button displays the agent's log. To expand, select the text area and press the **enter** button on the phone keyboard.

The Web Service contacts the NXTmonitor Master Server every 30 seconds for status update. You should keep this in mind when clicking the **Refresh** button.

Display the login page

Display the agents list

Display the agent log

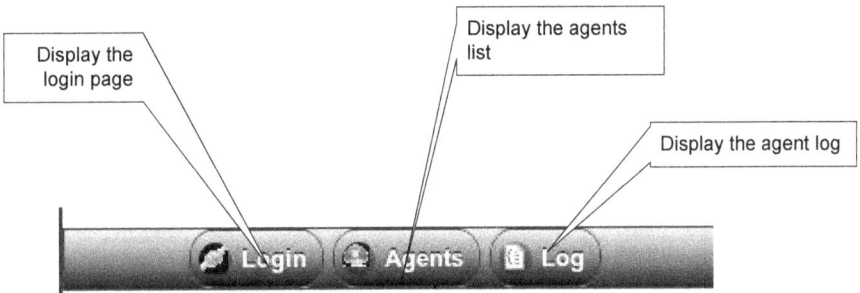

Chapter 7
Troubleshooting

This chapter describes trouble shooting techniques for your NXTmonitor application management system. The first section describes debugging broker error conditions encountered by NXTmonitor, as well as resolution tips. The other section describes typical errors and possible resolutions.

- "Debugging Broker errors" on page 144.

- "Problems a NXTera Distributed Application" on page 145.

- "Licensing errors:" on page 150.

- "Errors Starting NXTmonitor:" on page 151.

- "Console Login errors:" on page 154.

- "Unable to Connect / Problem loading page:" on page 155.

- "NXTmonitor Console not updating:" on page 156.

- "Logs" on page 157.

Debugging Broker errors

If you encounter errors after entering your configuration in NXTmonitor and starting it up, look at the broker log to see what error you are getting. If your broker port is in use, try a different port number. Any unused port between 2048 and 32767 should work. On a UNIX machine, you can find out if a port is in use by entering the following command:

```
netstat -a | grep port_num
```

If a line including the port you specified prints to the screen, then the port is in use. If you receive no response, then the port is free.

The port number for the broker is specified in the broker's environment file. Edit the broker environment file, save your changes to the environment file, and then make two more copies of it, called server.env and client.env. In each copy, specify a different file in the NXT_LOG variable. The log file specified in broker.env will be used by your Broker, while the other log files will be used by the server and client, as specified.

Example

The environment file included with your example files looks like this:

```
NXT_BROKER=193.1.1.60,7800
NXT_DEBUGLEVEL=DEBUG,DEBUG
NXT_LOG=broker.log
```

These settings indicate that a high level of debugging information will be written to a file in the current directory called broker.log, and that the Broker will be listening at port number 7800 on machine 193.1.1.60. We recommend that you modify the NXT_DEBUGLEVEL setting to DEBUG, DEBUG if you are having problems setting up your application's produc-tion environment in NXTmonitor. This setting will write the maximum amount of information to the log files to help you debug the problem.

Problems a NXTera Distributed Application

There can be many reasons why your distributed application is dying caus-ing a recycling (starting, then stopping and re-starting). For now, to verify that everything is working correctly, make sure that your client and server executables - their environment files - in the same directory. If it cannot be properly debugged within NXTmonitor, try executing the commands you have entered in a command line. From the directoy you have specified for the broker, start up the Broker:

```
rpcbroker -e broker.env -bg        for a UNIX server
```

This command starts the Broker as a background process. The Broker reads the specified environment file and then listens for connections at the port specified in the file.

Start your Server

Start the server you are having problems with in the directory you specified for it. Make sure the environment file exists and the executable is either in the path or in that directory. Here is an example of the basicsrv startup command:

```
basicsrv -e server.env -bg        for a UNIX server
```

This command starts the server as a background process. The server locates the Broker by reading the environment file, and then registers with the Bro-ker as an available server.

Start a Test Client

If you have constructed a test client, start it up at a command line by typing it on the command line to test the server (e.g. - for basicsrv client:

```
cclient
```

This command starts up the client, which prompts you for the environment file and then contacts the Broker for the names and locations of servers capable of fulfilling its requests. It then prompts you for input. Follow the instructions to see your distributed application in action.

Try rpcdebug

If you don't have a test client, start up **rpcdebug** utility (universal client) to test your new server:

```
rpcdebug
```

1. Select the Set Environment File option under the Environment tab and browse for a valid environment file to use for testing.

2. Next, click the Load Interface File under the File tab.

   This will bring up a file search window. Select the definition file (.def) which contains the description of the server you are testing with your test client. Select `basicsrv.def`.

3. All the functions associated with that interface will appear in the Remote Methods window.

4. Then double click on an individual function (add or lower2upper) in the remote methods window. In the input parameters window, enter values to send into the function. Then click on the run icon or select "Execute Remote Method" under the Run tab.

   It may take a few seconds the first time, but in a moment the "Output Parameters" window fills with the value returned by the function.

5. Now change your inputs or try the other function. When you click "Execute Remote Method", the response comes back almost instantaneously. This is because the client stub in rpcdebug stores the list of

available servers internally, so that it only queries the Broker on the first RPC, or when it cannot find an appropriate server.

Figure: 8.1 rpcdebug Main Window

6. You're finished!

    So now take a break, and pat yourself on the back for completing your
    first distributed application!

Appendix A - Errors

This section shows some of the errors discovered in testing and some of the typical problems that can occur. For each error, an explanation of the error is given and a resolution or possible causes for the problem.

Licensing errors:

This is a typical screen you will get on Windows if you attempt to start NXTmonitor without a valid license. This is caused by several things, but most likely the license file is corrupted, missing, or does not have the correct read permissions (Linux). To resolve this issue, download the license and insert in the license directory in the NXTmonitor_Server license directory.

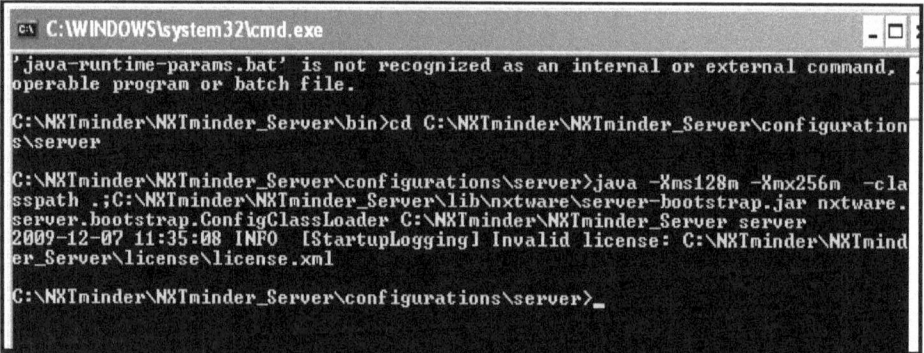

Errors Starting NXTmonitor:

If NXTmonitor stops running, and the highlighted message appears, it means that you <u>do not currently have Java 1.6 installed</u>. Install Java 1.6 and try again.

Errors starting Console:

If you are unable to start the console, go to the NXTmonitor Console directory and view the error log. Here is an example of one error:

In this case, the user failed to start up the Master Server or the Agent and the console is unable to connect (because they are not up).

Server errors:

In some cases the master server does not come up and after several minutes of Master Server retries it cannot establish database connectivity. This is usually the result of stale IORs. Under normal conditions, this does not usually happen.

Go to the NXTmonitor iors directory (in NXTmonitor_Server/configurations/server/tomcat) and delete all the IORS.

Console Login errors:

Sometimes there are errors displayed in the console window when attempting to login with a username and password. Here is an example of this error:

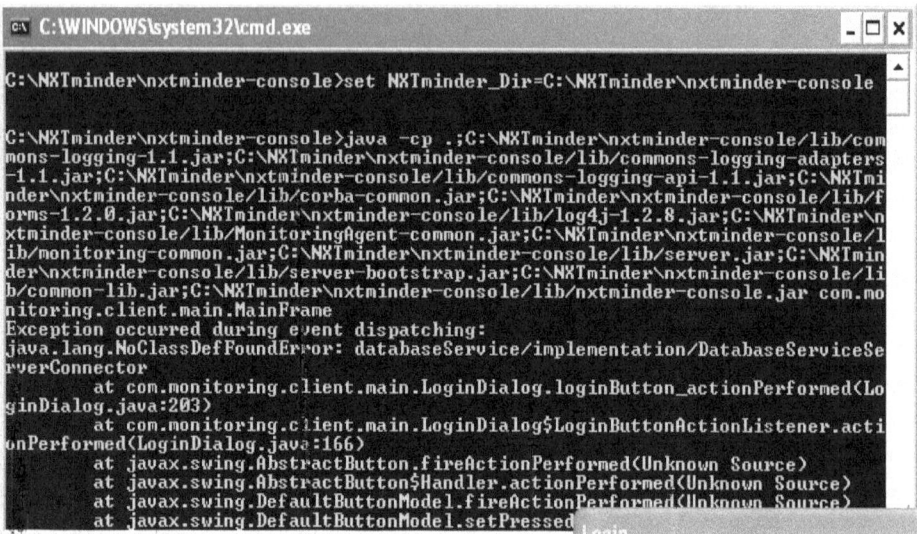

There is currently no resolution for these errors and they do not cause any adverse affects on NXTmonitor other than to fill up the log files with errors.

Unable to Connect / Problem loading page:

If you are trying to bring up the administrator browser to add users, you may get this message:

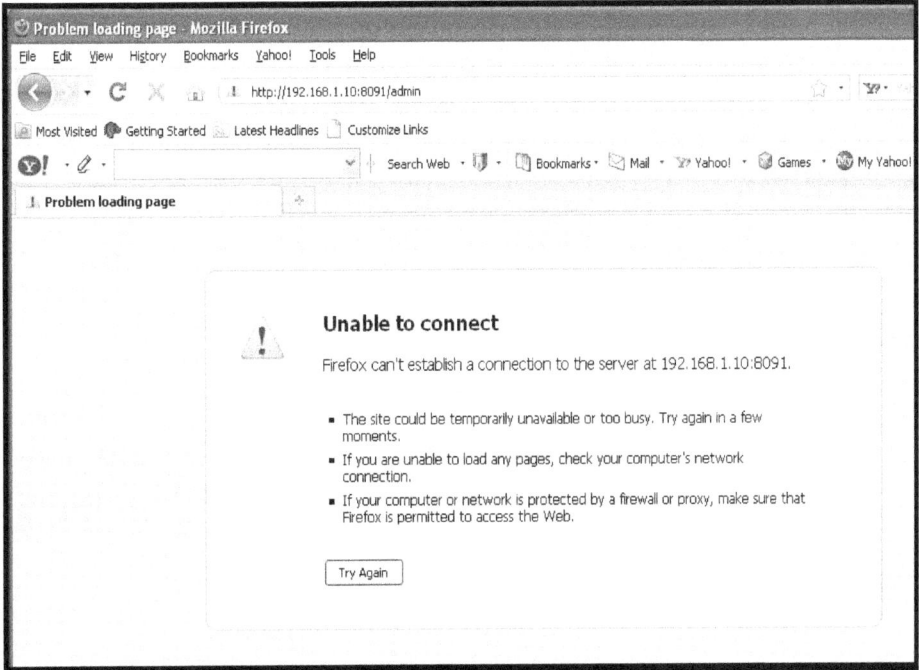

The possible answers to this problem are:

1. You have the wrong IP address for the Server.

2. You have not started the Master Server.

3. You have network issues reaching your Master Server.

NXTmonitor Console not updating:

If you have changed a configuration setting and the change is not reflected in the GUI, you should wait 30 seconds for the database to be updated. Configuration changes are made to the database, which may not necessarily reside on the same computer as your NXTmonitor Console. In order to make sure the Console displays correct information, changes are not made until successful update is received from the database.

You can force a refresh of the statuses by clicking the **Refresh** toolbar button.

You can force a reload of the different configurations by clicking the **Reload** toolbar button.

In order to make sure the Console displays correct information, changes are not made until successful update is received from the database. For more information on how to tune this parameter, see the Performance section in Managing Objects.

Logs

Accessing the Agent log

To access the agent log, select the agent node and right-click.

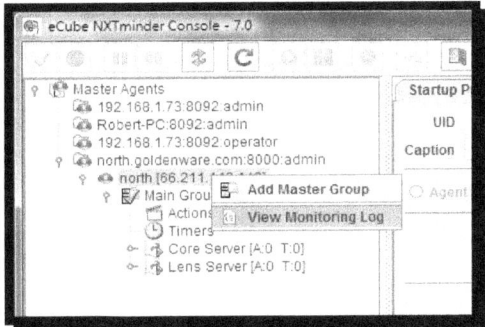

Accessing a launcher log file

You can access a log file generated by a launcher component by creating an environment variable named **"log_file"**.

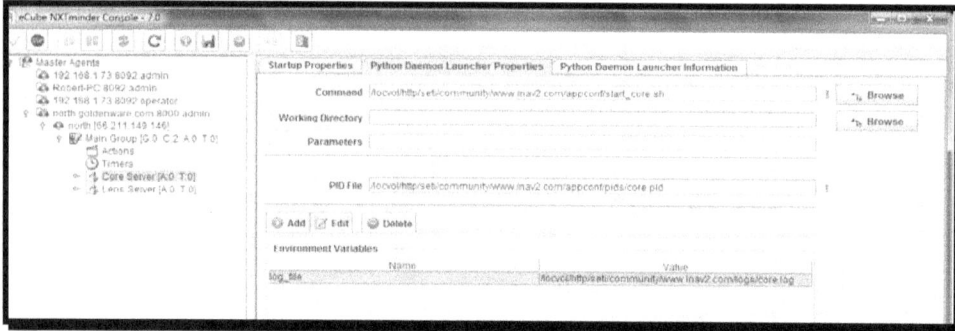

To view the log file, select the launcher object and right-click. Select **View Component Log**.

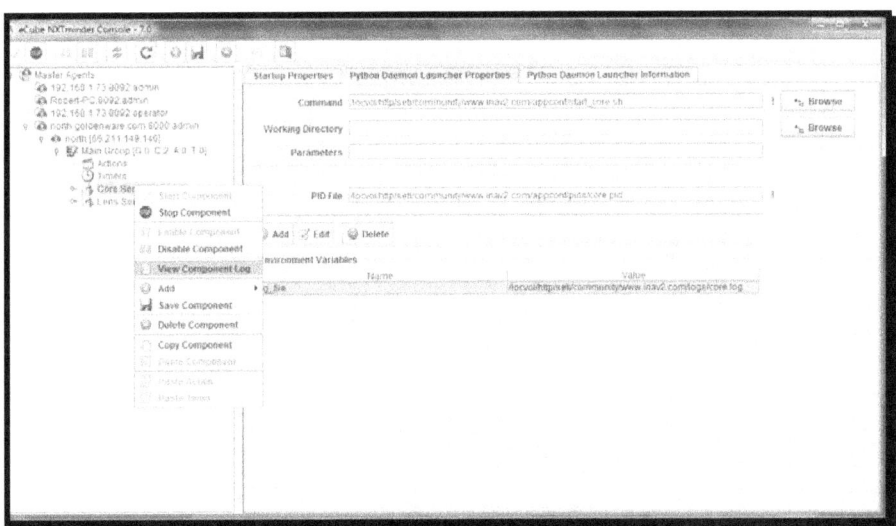